RAW TALKS WITH WISDOM

MIKE PASCHALL

NOT YOUR GRANDMA'S DEVO

volume 3
JULY, AUGUST, SEPTEMBER

RAW TALKS WITH WISDOM - *Not Your Grandma's Devo*
Volume 3 - (July, August, & September).

Copyright © 2013, 2018 by Michael D. Paschall.

All rights reserved. No part of this book may be reproduced or stored in a retrieval system, or transmitted in any form or by any means—electronic, mechanical, photocopying, recording, or otherwise, without the written permission of owner.

FIRST EDITION

ISBN: 978-0-578-43990-7

Cover & Title Page: Jon C. Egan

EVERY TRIBE INTERNATIONAL
Colorado Springs, Colorado

www.everytribeinternational.org
mike@mikepaschall.com

CONTENTS

Preface v

Dedication ix

JULY 1 - 55

AUGUST 59 - 112

SEPTEMBER 115 - 166

Endnotes 167

Resources & Other Helps 169

Acknowledgements 173

Author 177

PREFACE

HEY! Thank you so much for giving **RAW TALKS WITH WISDOM – *Not Your Grandma's Devo*** a whirl! It's an honor and a blessing to have you along for the ride. Before we get started, I thought it would be helpful to give you an idea of what this thing is all about.

FOUNDATIONS

Setting aside time every day for a devotional is probably one of the best disciplines I was ever encouraged to implement into my daily life. It has provided me countless connections with the Lord.

For the past 35 years, I have primarily read devotionals by two men, Dr. James Sidlow Baxter and Oswald Chambers. I was introduced to Dr. Baxter in 1978 by my first real spiritual mentor: Dr. H. D. McCarty. I heard Brother Sidlow speak on more than one occasion. He was already in his late '70s by the time I was introduced to his written work. I will always be thankful for **AWAKE MY HEART**. I learned so much from the meditations in that devotional.

Our friends, Earl and Barbara Patrick, gave me my first copy of **MY UTMOST FOR HIS HIGHEST** by Oswald Chambers when I was ordained in April 1986. I still use that same copy. I can't begin to describe the blessing that devotional has been to me. Chambers' revelations are amazing, especially considering he was only 43 years old when he died in 1917. His wife, Biddy, compiled transcripts and notes that eventually evolved into **UTMOST**, first published in 1927. I am forever in debt to them both for what was spoken, captured, and put into print for all of us to benefit.

MY DESIRE

My prayer is that the Lord will speak to you through **RAW TALKS WITH WISDOM – *Not Your Grandma's Devo***. I have always gained wisdom and perspective by reading scripture and devotionals, but more important to me has been how the Holy Spirit tailors each lesson to fit my life. It doesn't really mean anything unless we can practically apply truth to the joys and tears of the now.

If all you come away with after working through these devotionals is more knowledge, then I'd have to really evaluate if it was all worth it. I would encourage you to take it to another level, beyond mere theology and theory, into the realms of practical reality--stuff you can wear, taste, and feel. I want you to know He gave you revelation!

MY VISION

It's simple. Do this devotional the way you would do any other devotional. But what I really want is for these daily lessons to stimulate journaling (which is the reason for the **"In the Pages"** questions at the end of each day). I would encourage you to make an appointment to meet with the Lord each day, and then stick with it. Daily appointments can become healthy habits in a relatively short period of time. Pick a time each day that "works" best for you, and make Him a priority!

I want the material to stick with you. I want you to chew on it throughout your day. I want you to discuss it over coffee with a friend or colleague. Stuff like that. My ultimate prayer is that ***RAW TALKS WITH WISDOM – Not Your Grandma's Devo*** adds value to your quiet times with the Lord!

Like I said, I want you to do this devotional the way you do devotionals. But here is the method I would use to tackle each day:

First, read the **entire chapter** of Proverbs for that day. If the day is June 11, then read all of Proverbs chapter 11.

Then read the focus verses that begin each devo.

Third, read the devotional itself.

Fourth, journal your responses to the **In The Pages** questions at the end, along with anything else you feel compelled to write about. Get yourself a good leather-bound journal! Your thoughts and prayers deserve a proper container.

Lastly, spend some time in prayer and meditation.

That is the vision.

I sincerely hope the Holy Spirit will speak to you through these devotionals and give you things to write about in your journal. I also hope these devotionals will get you in the habit of reading through all of Proverbs twelve times in one year. For as long as I have been soaking in Proverbs, I have found a surprise almost every time! A new perspective, a nugget of value, something I've never seen before. It has to be the Holy Spirit that does that, and so far, I love the process!

WHY *RAW TALKS WITH WISDOM* – *Not Your Grandma's Devo*?

It dawned on me one day that our relationships with the Lord should always be raw. I was stuck in the rut of religious activity for far too long! What I have with Him now feels very real, relaxed, and extremely relevant.

I live and work in a culture that is filled with young and old ideas. I have definitely mellowed over the years and learned how to slow down. I think this season is teaching me to be more focused on the stuff that actually counts. To say it, whatever "it" really is, without apology and with serious conviction.

I'm not a theologian. I know that. So there is no use in my trying to be one. I'm a weird mixture of stuff with a rich experience of failure and profound grace. ***RAW TALKS WITH WISDOM – Not Your Grandma's Devo*** is a title that feels like me. It gives me permission to be myself and say things like I really do.

I know the angels won't sing along to every single one of these devotionals for you. But maybe, just maybe, some of it will help someone, somewhere, turn and embrace the **RAW** truth of God's wisdom.

Michael D. Paschall
2013

For those who follow.

Flying Squirrels

July 1
Proverbs 1

"Indeed, it is useless to spread the baited net in the sight of any bird; but they lie in wait for their own blood; they ambush their own lives." Proverbs 1:17-18, NASB

For about 11 verses, Solomon spins a web composed of the treacheries of falling into the enticement of fools. Any child would appreciate the simplicity of this teaching.

Most of us learned how to trap animals in one way or another at a very early age. Using a pit, a cage, or a net, we'd somehow camouflage the trap, present the bait, and prepare the springing mechanism.

I used to run traps as a kid (with my BFF) to catch raccoons and possums near a creek just outside of where I grew up. Raccoons have a hard time passing up an open can of sardines or peanut butter. It's all great fun, and I guess for some cultures, it's still a necessary way to feed your family.

Someone recently sent me a hilarious video of a contraption some guy put together for the pesky squirrels on his back deck. It's a modified skeet launcher that he baits with peanuts. Once the squirrel settles on the device to enjoy his free treats, the guy pulls a cord from a hidden location and the squirrel is launched out into the wild blue yonder! It's a squirrel that flies, not to be confused with a flying squirrel. Some people have way too much time on their hands. But, man! What great redneck entertainment!

Today's message is simple: even the birds (evidently not all squirrels) know enough to fly away when someone is setting an obvious trap. Anyone foolish enough to set a trap should be aware that they too could become a victim of their own device.

We love those stories, don't we? Where the bad guy sets a trap, or some scheme to harm another person, and the whole thing backfires on him? Unfortunately, it doesn't always work like that.

Let today's message land on you. We don't need to be influenced and enticed by schemers. Why? *"They ambush their own lives"*! The Hebrew word for *"ambush"* is **tsâphan** (prounounced *tsaw-fan'*); which *means "to* *hide or cover up, a spirit of hoarding; the denial and sabotage of one's own welfare."*

Steer clear of their ways, and you'll stay out of their nets.

In The Pages

When is the last time you got caught in the web of another person's spinning? Have you ever caught yourself in a scheme planned for another's demise? How long did it take you to figure out that the trap to injure or harm another was a bad idea?

The Paths of the Righteous

July 2
Proverbs 2

"That thou mayest walk in the way of good men, and keep the paths of the righteous." Proverbs 2:20, KJV

Hmmmmm... *"and keep the paths of the righteous."* What does that mean?

Proverbs 4:18 says, *"But the path of the righteous is like the light of dawn, that shines brighter and brighter until the full day"* (NASB).

Well, whatever it means, it must be good stuff! Let's dig a bit.

Today's verse is part of a three-verse package. I've singled this one out because I want to deal with it specifically. What is this *"path of the righteous?"*

I've been in church too long to ask this question in certain circles. Why? Because I know I'll get a quick list of qualifying works. You know—the rules, the dos and don'ts, the rights and wrongs.

These things throw insecure people and rejected saints into a tizzy of works and pious expressions for God and man's approval. I think we've got better news than this. But that freaks out the church.

The "good news" has a lot of *good news* in it... maybe more than we're comfortable with. So, instead of giving you a long list of things you can do to be on the *"paths of the righteous"*, how about we take a different direction?

Hebrews 11:6 says, *"And without faith it is impossible to please Him, for he who comes to God must believe that He is and that He is a rewarder of those who seek Him"* (NASB).

I know I'm not the brightest bulb on the planet, but it makes sense to me that if I've got something inside of me that is actually *pleasing* to God, then it is probably considered *righteous* to the Lord, right?

With a little bit of reasoning, I feel certain that one of the elements of the *"paths of the righteous"* would involve *faith*!

Hebrews 6:11-12 says, *"And we desire that each one of you show the same diligence so as to realize the full assurance of hope until the end, so that you will not be sluggish, but imitators of those who through faith and patience inherit the promises"* (NASB).

There we hear it again! *"Through faith and patience we inherit"* the things that God has stored up for those who keep the *"paths of the righteous"*. I'm not sure if you caught it or not, but if you're going to live in *faith*, it's going to also require some *patience*.

God's timing and my timing don't usually mesh together too well. Staying in *faith* sometimes requires that I trust Him, even when I don't have what I want in my hands today! Still believing, still hoping, and still pursuing our God, even when we have nothing tangible in our possession, takes *patience*!

Faith is the great divider of the posers from the pursuers. It is what separates dead religion from true "Spirit"-uality. Surely, that is also a part of the *"paths of the righteous"*!

In The Pages

When is the last time you asked God for something that was totally beyond your reach? If your request isn't met on your timetable, how willing are you to continue to pray and ask in faith anyway? Build your faith. Read Hebrews 11. Be encouraged!

Booby *What?*

July 3
Proverbs 3

"Wise living gets rewarded with honor; stupid living gets the booby prize."
Proverbs 3:35, MSG

Yeah, this was too good to pass up today. Peterson must have had a good laugh when he scribbled out the words *"booby prize"* in his original drafts! Ha! Yeah, yeah, I know we usually think of "mammary glands" when we hear the word booby, but it's also another word for a dunce (*a person considered to be incapable of learning*).

A *"booby prize"* is what's given to last place finishers in a contest, as a token of acknowledgment. Dr. Peterson is absolutely right. Stupid living *does* get the *booby prize*. There is absolutely no argument here.

On the other hand,

manifesting wisdom helps creates an environment for honor.

Recently, I read something in some religious propaganda that I found not only bothersome, but also extremely shortsighted. You can make your own assessment.

The statement implied that *honor* is an "Old Testament" concept, thus triumphed by grace, a "New Testament" concept. Honestly, I don't know if that individual would defend that statement today, but I disagree wholeheartedly!

Honor is a *wisdom* concept,

and neither *honor*, nor grace, can be pigeonholed as "Old Testament" or "New Testament" concepts. Jesus was all over *honor*, and the Apostles' teaching is steeped in the concept. Paul was particularly fascinated with teachings of *honor*, especially toward his spiritual son Timothy (1 Timothy 5:3, 5:17, 6:1; 2 Timothy 2:20-21).

Peter said, *"Honor all people, love the brotherhood, fear God, honor the king"* (1 Peter 2:17, NASB). The power of *honor* is that it requires us to make some choices, just like we have to make choices in order to release grace.

Grace isn't religious "pixie dust" from Disneyland.

We are partakers of His grace because God made a costly choice to prefer, and *honor,* our need for reconciliation. Grace is supernatural. It's eternal! To *honor* properly, to give properly, to prefer properly, to serve properly, to worship properly, to use the gifts properly, to live in true covenant unity (formalized by ritual or not), to disciple properly, to be a proper disciple—all require the supernatural infusion of grace!

But it's not one over the other, and I'm not convinced you can separate it out cleanly. Maybe one is *how* we live, and the other is *why* we live. Maybe?

True *honor* is a by-product of wisdom. Wisdom is from the Godhead. It knows no time, nor dispensation. *Honor* has always been a part of the package, from the beginning of time. No booby prizes there.

In The Pages

Check out these verses: Ezra 9:8; Psalms 45:2, 84:11; Proverbs 4:1-9; Jeremiah 31:1-3. What is the common theme? How long has supernatural power, which enables people to be and do God's work, been around?

America the Beautiful

Fourth of July

It's a toss-up between the Fourth of July and Thanksgiving for my favorite holiday. There's less commercialism, and they're both exclusively American.

There's just something about the entire country coming together in gratitude for the blessing of living in this great land; celebrating the sharing of space with others whose lineages came together on ancient trails to build our common identity as Americans. And it came at a great price.

It is right that we celebrate and give thanks to God!

Have you ever checked out the lyrics to *America the Beautiful*? I mean all the lyrics? In 1883, the poet Katharine Lee Bates was moved to words as she rode up to the top of Pikes Peak by cog railroad. Two years later, she published the poem *Pikes Peak*, whose name later changed to *America*.

As the poem gained national popularity, it was put to music in 1904, thus our known rendition of *America the Beautiful* evolved. Today, let's soak in our patriotic heritage and all of God's goodness!

O beautiful for spacious skies,
For amber waves of grain,
For purple mountain majesties
Above the fruited plain!
America! America!
God shed his grace on thee
And crown thy good with brotherhood
From sea to shining sea!

O beautiful for pilgrim feet
Whose stern impassioned stress
A thoroughfare of freedom beat
Across the wilderness!
America! America!
God mend thine every flaw,
Confirm thy soul in self-control,
Thy liberty in law!

O beautiful for heroes proved
In liberating strife.
Who more than self their country loved
And mercy more than life!
America! America!
May God thy gold refine
Till all success be nobleness
And every gain divine!

O beautiful for patriot dream
That sees beyond the years
Thine alabaster cities gleam
Undimmed by human tears!
America! America!
God shed his grace on thee
And crown thy good with brotherhood
From sea to shining sea!

O beautiful for halcyon skies,
For amber waves of grain,
For purple mountain majesties
Above the enameled plain!
America! America!
God shed his grace on thee
Till souls wax fair as earth and air
And music-hearted sea!

O beautiful for pilgrims feet,
Whose stem impassioned stress
A thoroughfare for freedom beat
Across the wilderness!
America! America!
God shed his grace on thee
Till paths be wrought through
wilds of thought
By pilgrim foot and knee!

O beautiful for glory-tale
Of liberating strife
When once and twice,
for man's avail
Men lavished precious life!
America! America!
God shed his grace on thee
Till selfish gain no longer stain
The banner of the free!

O beautiful for patriot dream
That sees beyond the years
Thine alabaster cities gleam
Undimmed by human tears!
America! America!
God shed his grace on thee
Till nobler men keep once again
Thy whiter jubilee!

GOD BLESS THE UNITED STATES OF AMERICA!

Prison of Regret

July 5
Proverbs 5

"And thou mourn at the last, when thy flesh and thy body are consumed, and say, How have I hated instruction, and my heart despised reproof; and have not obeyed the voice of my teachers, nor inclined mine ear to them that instructed me! I was almost in all evil in the midst of the congregation and assembly." Proverbs 5:11-14, KJV

"If the Lord had not been my help, my soul would soon have dwelt in the abode of silence." Psalms 94:17, NASB

(Read all of Proverbs 5 today. It sets proper tone and context.)

If we're not careful, we can slip into thinking that keeping the precepts of Wisdom is all about having the right answers. Nothing could be further from the truth.

It doesn't hurt to have some data stored inside of us, but our walk with Wisdom is about having an understanding of how to live fully alive and in sync with God's purpose and blessing. There should be a progression of confirmation that Lady Wisdom is good, she is *for* us, and she is all about adding value to our lives.

Wisdom isn't trying to restrict us but thrives to see our lives increase in peace, completed satisfaction, and rested contentment. A finish that is void of regret!

It's such a difficult concept for youth or the young at heart. We either don't appreciate the *"peaceful fruit of righteousness"* (Hebrews 12:11), or we can't handle restriction of any kind.

And some of us just plain ole have issues with authority.

Whatever the deal, Wisdom would really employ us to "get over ourselves," forgive our past, honor our present, and finish strong. Ah yes, the infamous "one day" (fuzzy and dim as it is to us) will eventually be our "today." We'll be glad we handled "now" with much more attentiveness.

For the sorrow that is according to the will of God produces a repentance without regret, leading to salvation, but the sorrow of the world produces death. For behold what earnestness this very thing, this godly sorrow, has produced in you: what vindication of yourselves, what indignation, what fear, what longing, what zeal, what avenging of wrong! In everything you demonstrated yourselves to be innocent in the matter (2 Corinthians 7:10-11, NASB).

Paul had rebuked, and wounded, the church in Corinth. But they listened to his insight and repented.

Beloved, repentance is a gift from God!

"Or do you think lightly of the riches of His kindness and tolerance and patience, not knowing that the kindness of God leads you to repentance?" (Romans 2:4, NASB).

They (the church) released their faults, plunged them under the blood of Christ, and bathed themselves in the forgiveness and restorative grace of the Lord! No matter what we've done in life, the same is available for you and for me!

We don't have to live in a prison of regret. We can be assured of our forgiveness—freed, and absolved from the sins of our past failures.

Life doesn't have to end in shame and regret! It just doesn't!

In The Pages

Read *Matthew 27:3-5* and *Acts 1:16-20*. What is the difference between "worldly" sorrow and "godly" sorrow? Do you think after the dust had settled, Judas could have been restored? Why or why not?

The Way of Life

July 6
Proverbs 6

"For the commandment is a lamp and the teaching is light; and reproofs for discipline are the way of life." Proverbs 6:23, NASB

"For sound advice is a beacon, good teaching is a light, moral discipline is a life path." Proverbs 6:23, MSG

"The precepts of the Lord are right, rejoicing the heart; the commandment of the Lord is pure, enlightening the eyes." Psalms 19:8, NASB

"Your word is a lamp to my feet and a light to my path." Psalms 119:105, NASB

I hope you caught yesterday's concept that Wisdom is more concerned with adding value to your life than just restricting it. While the guidance does include healthy doses of warning and correction, there are usually very specific examples of why some things are best avoided altogether.

The voice of Wisdom is so personal and so dialed in to the "big picture," we never get that *"because I said so"* approach. Today's proverb is a perfect example for us. We should feel like we're having a great talk with a loving parent.

I want us to focus on three things from today's text. First, look at the verses following today's proverb (verses 24-35). They begin with the words, *"To keep you."* In the original language, it means to *"place a hedge of thorns around you for protection."*

Yes, the thorny briars protect you, but they also remind you to take extreme caution with how you proceed. Considering the subject matter of those eleven verses that follow, I suggest we listen!

Secondly, *"lamp"* means the burner of light, but it also holds this idea of glistening. When we think of glisten, we see oily skin or sweat—something that is *on* us, because it came from *within* us.

The usage of this word *"light"* in the Hebrew is *illumination*, but it can include all elements of luminary, including clarity and happiness. Wisdom tells us constantly that if we get God's truth in us, it will surface when needed. Its truth will shine brightly and clarify our paths with a resolution that dispenses the confusion of darkness and shadows. It's a happy way to live!

Thirdly, *"reproofs"* is **tôwkachath** (pronounced *to-kakh´-ath*); and it means *"correction by words and reasoning."* The love in a relationship is what allows for communication and legit feedback.

It's something different than you just getting your butt kicked by an old person.

In today's culture, it's rare for people to pursue and embrace real discipleship or mentoring. Discipleship starts with a paradigm that teaches us to spiritually self-govern and do so from sanctified reason and experiential wisdom.

The Holy Spirit is all about this and will help us if we can take the *reproofs* and *discipline* without being offended. Wisdom says this IS *"the way of life."*

In The Pages

What part of today's lessons spoke clearest to you? Why? How much of the logos (word) is in you? Do you have a plan for increasing this discipline? How would you help a new Christian gain appreciation for studying and reading the Bible?

The Slain Many

July 7
Proverbs 7

"For she has brought down many fatally wounded, and all those she has slain are many." Proverbs 7:26, NET

"She" is the adulterer. I'm not making excuses for her, but we need to understand that we are dealing with a person who is under the influence of darkness.

Whether it's spiritual bondage or character deficiency, this person has been through some stuff that forged her development into this role. The thing I noticed today is that *she* (the demonic spirit that influences adultery; which is neither male nor female) preys upon the *fatally wounded*.

Not to say it can't bring down the strong, but the *"wounded"* are easier targets. Once it has its *wounded* victim in its lair, it's only a matter of time before there is one more to add to the *slain many*.

This is another one of those devos where I've spent most of today thinking about it. This thought of the slain many is heavy. Too heavy.

Men of warfare are familiar with the term, *coup de grâce*. It's a French term meaning, *"blow of mercy."*

Men (or animals) severely injured in battle were mercifully killed, either by their enemy or their own, to end their suffering. It was usually a blow to the back of the head, or a sword, or a gunshot to the heart.

The Japanese Samurai had a similar arrangement with the Bushido honor code, followed by a ceremony to absolve the Samurai from shame or falling into enemy hands (Seppuku).

He'd plunge a knife into his own midsection, slice it open, and then extend his neck to be beheaded by another Samurai. Honor restored.

Maybe we don't see as much of this anymore because modern technology and resources allow us to evacuate the wounded, and render aid quickly. But back in the day, this was a legitimate expression of grace and mercy.

The *spirit of adultery*, on the other hand, feasts on the wounded. It looks for the weak, the exhausted, the bored, those who feel used up, unappreciated, discontented, and ignored.

These are regular people, just like you and me who, for some reason, have either stopped talking, stopped pursuing, or are no longer being romanced by the one who vowed *"until death do us part."*

"For she has brought down many fatally wounded", are some of the saddest words ever written! The kind of killing *she* does is NO act of mercy.

She has no regard for family, children, or the precious future of inheritance.

She does not care what she kills today or what she sets into motion in a lineage.

She doesn't care that real generational traits will manifest in the natural and ultimately have to be dealt with in the spirit.

She just doesn't care.

There is no one to judge here. If your parents are divorced, give them grace and mercy. Take care of your own house. Protect your relationships. Love your mate extravagantly! The *spirit of adultery* can smell blood and wounded decay.

Don't let those smells emanate from you!

In The Pages

If a great defense is the best offense against the enemy, what are you doing to protect the love fires in your marriage (Sorry singles)? Are you still creating sexual opportunities and memories with your mate? Are you still proving your love, and are you willing to show and communicate that truth?

We've Got To Dance

July 8
Proverbs 8

"I love those who love me; and those who diligently seek me will find me. Riches and honor are with me, enduring wealth and righteousness." Proverbs 8:17-18, NKJV

"May he kiss me with the kisses of his mouth! For your love is better than wine. Your oils have a pleasing fragrance, your name is like purified oil; therefore the maidens love you. Draw me after you and let us run together! The king has brought me into his chambers." Song of Solomon 1:2-4, NASB

Today's Proverb has the alluring fragrance of a righteous seduction! The Hebrew understanding of the *love* expressed here suggests a definitive sexual component. No, I'm not saying that Wisdom is sexual. I'm referring to the seductive element of Wisdom's goodness.

As we move towards Lady Wisdom, as we desire to go deeper with her, she responds and gives us more of herself in return. *"Those who diligently seek me will find me."* Yeah, baby!

The word for *"find"* is **mâtsâ'** (pronounced maw-tsaw') meaning, *"to come forth, to appear or reveal an existence."* The imagery is so rich. Wisdom, the lover (*the sensual lover, not like how we love buttered popcorn at the* *movies*), makes herself available, and we respond accordingly!

We take the bait of a righteous seduction.

As we move towards the ever-deepening relationship and eventual consummation, we discover that she is continually revealing more and more of herself as we go deeper together in a reciprocating offer-and-response arrangement. It's a beautiful picture, as displayed in Song of Solomon 1:2-4 (see above).

The Groom makes a move. The Bride responds. The Groom makes another move towards that response. The Bride, likewise, moves in responsive synchronicity. Thus, the dance of passion and love evolves.

Much like the maiden in this Song of Solomon passage, we have a means of approach to a person of resource and provision. Relationship and consummation afford us full access to the vastness of Lady Wisdom's kingdom. *"Riches and honor... enduring wealth and righteousness."*

Such a treasury at our disposal, and all we have to do is dance!

Other than (maybe) Leviticus, the book of Proverbs may be the most overlooked book in scripture. Discovering the vast glory of Wisdom's instruction only confirms her real love for us.

It is another sensational display of God's affection for His people. And quite honestly, any intentional move towards Proverb's wisdom will constantly yield another word from the Spirit that directly applies to your life!

It is amazing how often it works out that way! But we've got to dance the dance.

We have to take her seductive hints. We have to be willing to be drawn in by all of her charms and desires.

A lover she is, and a lover she will be. So let's dance.

In The Pages

Have you felt the seductive charms of Proverbs? If not, what book in Scripture has your heart and eyes? If you struggle with Proverbs, what is the complication? Did today's lesson help open your heart towards our dance with Wisdom? Why or why not?

Long Life

July 9
Proverbs 9

"It's through me, Lady Wisdom, that your life deepens, and the years of your life ripen. Proverbs 9:11, MSG

"For by me your days will be multiplied, and years of life will be added to you." Proverbs 9:11, NASB

What we're reaping here is the byproduct of: Proverbs 9:10, *"The fear of the Lord is the beginning of wisdom, and the knowledge of the Holy One is understanding"* (NASB). What a promise!

It's a promise we see several times throughout this magnificent book:

"The fear of the Lord prolongs life, but the years of the wicked will be shortened" (Proverbs 10:27, NASB).

"The fear of the Lord is a fountain of life, that one may avoid the snares of death" (Proverbs 14:27, NASB).

"The fear of the Lord leads to life, so that one may sleep satisfied, untouched by evil" (Proverbs 19:23, NASB).

Moses also considered the love of the Lord and His commandments as life-giving (Deuteronomy 4:40). Although not everyone who loves God ends up living a long life, it might be fair to say that there is at least the potential for that *deepened ripeness* that Peterson suggests.

It is wisdom to pack our lives full of the Lord's presence, and thus the fullness of His Spirit and experience! A fully alive life, actively engaged, *until every knee bows and every tongue confesses that Jesus Christ is Lord!* (Philippians 2:10-11)

So, are you up for that?

Seriously? I wonder sometimes if we are.

I saw a tweet last night from an old friend who has high influence in his denomination. He said, "Come Lord Jesus. NOW!" I stared at it for the longest time. I thought, *"I wonder if everyone in that massive church where he pastors would be "ok"* (interpret that however you will) *with the Lord's rapturous return today?"*

My second thought was more of my own internal dialogue: *"The frikk'n planet is covered with people who have yet to know or experience the love of God. It can't be over now! We have to tell them, get them a message, and do something with the truth we possess! If the promise of living in honor of our God adds years and value to our very existence, why are we in such a hurry to rapture out of here? Heaven waits on His perfect timing. I know we'll go there some day—but probably not today. Why this selfish-inward plea to escape our responsibility and privilege to be witnesses to those who don't know Him?"*

Jesus said, *"Go therefore and make disciples of all the nations, baptizing them in the name of the Father and the Son and the Holy Spirit, teaching them to observe all that I commanded you; and lo, I am with you always, even to the end of the age"* (Matthew 28:19-20, NASB).

It's the foundation of all evangelical methodology!

Why would anyone ask for an escape until the gospel (the Good News that God loves us) has been preached to everyone? There are lots of people in this world who do not know what HE did to reconcile us to himself! We still have lots of "Good News" to give away.

Granted, bringing the Kingdom of Light into the darkness of this world is tough work! Fighting religious demons gets wearisome. But the whole earth groans for the workers of His righteousness to bring the refreshing knowledge of Living Water.

Can we stop bitching and moaning about our circumstances and get on with bringing the GOOD NEWS of the Kingdom? Our Savior and Champion didn't defeat hell only to provide us with an early check out!

In The Pages

Long life! Come on, let's prophesy: **LONG LIFE!** A full lifetime of serving our Lord and King! Bringing the Kingdom, reaping and sowing in the great harvest of souls! Prophesy it with me!

Sooner or Later

July 10
Proverbs 10

"He who walks with integrity walks securely, but he who perverts his ways will become known." Proverbs 10:9, NKJV

"Honesty lives confident and carefree, but Shifty is sure to be exposed." Proverbs 10:9, MSG

The man of integrity walks securely, but he who takes crooked paths will be found out." Proverbs 10:9, NIV

The definitive tones of *"will become known," "sure to be exposed,"* and *"will be found out"* is what specifically grabbed my attention today. I think we've already got this figured out when it comes to "big" people and companies exploiting their power in reckless ways.

People with an evil nature do evil things. We expect that they'll *eventually* be publicly exposed. But at the same time, I think we tend to overlook these same issues in our own simple lives.

Sometimes we realize that we have been askew with our attitudes or with the way we have treated someone. Then the Spirit comes, turns the light on our errors, and we're invited to repent, change our mind and our heart, and be restored back to a straight path.

It doesn't always have to be some big, newsworthy event. Most of the time, it's the little stuff—the stuff no one ever knows about except you and the Lord.

I can't even tell you the number of times the Lord has spoken to me during my quiet time about how I treated my wife, spoke to my kids, or handled a friend, colleague, or brother or sister of the faith. And if I'm being really stubborn, I'll get a disturbing dream that will dramatically challenge what I'm ignoring.

Yes, this kind of exposure with the Lord is quite humbling. *Conviction, exposure, shame*, and *regret* all create a mighty thirst for forgiveness and the sweet grace of the Lord! We get to see what He could see all along. Love demands that He shine light on our shifty shadows.

We never expect such crooked ways and perverted paths in our spiritual communities, but unfortunately, things aren't always as they appear.

Jesus was extremely transparent with his disciples about what they could expect from the sons of Abraham. Discipleship aimed towards the lost sheep of Israel had some drawbacks (Matthew 10:10-15). The old-line power brokers would always have issues with new methods and the relational aspects of real discipleship (Matthew 10:16-23).

But Jesus assured them that their tactics and false paradigms would eventually be exposed for the ultimate shallowness they really were.

He said, *"Therefore do not fear them, for there is nothing concealed that will not be revealed, or hidden that will not be known"* (Matthew 10:26, NASB).

Paul ran into similar issues as he instructed his spiritual son:

"The sins of some people are blatant and march them right into court. The sins of others don't show up until much later. The same with good deeds. Some you see right off, but none are hidden forever" (1 Timothy 5:24-25, MSG).

Just because a ministry is large, with slick marketing and impressive websites, doesn't necessarily mean that things are done with integrity and forthright tactics.

Ask yourself, how do they really handle the sheep or the people who work for then? Do they deliver what they promise? Do the people who work for them, respect them? How open and transparently does the leadership live in front of those they lead?

In The Pages

Take a moment and read 2 Samuel 12. Do you need a Nathan to stand beside you before you are able to see what the Lord sees, or do you pick up on more subtle hints? When do you best hear? How do you best hear?

Just A Matter Of Time

July 11
Proverbs 11

"The desire of the righteous is only good, but the expectation of the wicked is wrath." Proverbs 11:23, NASB

"But because of your stubbornness and unrepentant heart you are storing up wrath for yourself in the day of wrath and revelation of the righteous judgment of God, who will render to each person according to his deeds: to those who by perseverance in doing good seek for glory and honor and immortality, eternal life; but to those who are selfishly ambitious and do not obey the truth, but obey unrighteousness, wrath and indignation. There will be tribulation and distress for every soul of man who does evil, of the Jew first and also of the Greek, but glory and honor and peace to everyone who does good, to the Jew first and also to the Greek. For there is no partiality with God." Romans 2:5-11, NASB

Look at the second part of today's Proverb: *"... but the expectation of the wicked is wrath"*. What a depressing thought! Let's look closer.

What does *"expectation"* mean? Webster's defines it as *"a strong belief that something is going to happen in the future."* I think we can all agree on that definition.

But the word Solomon used was **tiqvâh** (pronounced *tik-vaw'*) literally meaning, *"cord,"* or *"the thing that ties or binds you to what is ahead."* There are so many applications here; it's hard to know where to start.

The point is that the *"wicked"* (*people who know what they're doing is wrong, and morally jeopardize themselves and others anyway*) already have a sense inside their *knower* that something bad is looming in their future.

It might be a lame example, but if you're a person who runs drugs or guns illegally, you already know how the story is going to end. Maybe you'll live to see tomorrow, or maybe you won't. But sooner or later the gig will be up, and it's not going to be pretty! It's just a matter of time.

The word for *"wrath"* is **ebrâh** (pronounced *eb-raw'*) meaning, *"an outburst of passion; hot, ugly, destructive passion."* Whether it is the *wrath* of God or the *wrath* of man, it matters not.

The *wicked* decide to take the risk anyway. Even if things are going well and we're profiting substantially, we still know, down in our deeps, it's going to end badly.

What we probably don't realize is that this same spirit can be efficiently cloaked inside of religious pride.

Would you find it interesting that Paul, speaking to Christians in Rome, points out *selfish ambition* as a part of this *wickedness* package?

"But to those who are selfishly ambitious and do not obey the truth, but obey unrighteousness, wrath and indignation. **There will be** *tribulation and distress for every soul of man who does evil, of the Jew first and also of the Greek"* (Romans 2:8, NASB). This is just... –sigh-

The KJV renders it as *"contentious"*. Honestly, the current Church reeks of this factious crap. As long as our "being right" is our main objective, our lives will be consumed with proving and defending our own points and positions, while simultaneously tearing down our brothers and sisters with words and caustic attitudes.

We shouldn't be surprised to find the word *wrath* in the same context. Yeah, it's just a matter of time.

In The Pages

How do you define *selfish ambition*? Can you explain how it operates in the Body of Christ? What kind of destruction have you seen it bear?

Bringeth Forth Favour

July 12
Proverbs 12

"The good bringeth forth favour from Jehovah, and the man of wicked devices He condemneth." Proverbs 12:2, YLT

Although this translation sets us back over a hundred years, it is the one translation I felt comes really close to conveying the essence of what Solomon is trying to say here. Let's break it down a bit and take a closer look.

The negative side first. The *"man of wicked devices"* gives us a clear indication of why the Lord condemns, or at least declares that this man's ways are messed up. Basically, this guy has placed all of his trust in his own ability to make a plan or scheme. It's not that the plan is necessarily wicked (it surely can be), but this guy's heart is oblivious to any need for God to be involved.

Ultimately, it's the pride of life!

Which is *"a total disregard for spiritual influence and the ultimate decision to do it my way, no matter what"*.

The *"condemneth"* part means that God disagrees with this way. It doesn't mean He has already sentenced the guy, but He might strongly disapprove of what is going on because it's contrary to what He knows is best for all of us.

I like this translation specifically for the words, *"bringeth forth favour"*. The NASB uses the word, *obtain*. When I hear, *obtain*, I think, *"receive."* I know that's not what it means, but that's what I hear.

Picture a little child at a lemonade stand, hands cupped, waiting for patrons to hand over their coins. Actually, *favour* can be like that. But here, the *good man* has vested himself into the flow of God. He's put a straw into the malt of God's person and tapped in to the anointing and ointment of God's goodness. He sucks, he draws, and he pulls the very substance of *favour* into, and over, his life!

I can't help but think about what happened to people who personally encountered the "Second Adam," the man, and firstborn witness of God (Romans 8:29). Jesus was absolute *favour* and His father's delight.

A friend of mine says, "Where Jesus showed up, health broke out!" It's so true. He was a game-changer in every way.

The people Jesus engaged found themselves cheek-to-cheek with the supernatural substance of heaven. Most of these people were in rough shape. It was all they could do to cup their hands and hope He looked their way.

But there was one woman who did more than cup her hands.

"And a woman who had a hemorrhage for twelve years, and could not be

healed by anyone, came up behind Him and touched the fringe of His cloak, and immediately her hemorrhage stopped" (Luke 8:43-44, NASB).

There was something about her that brought *"forth favour from Jehovah"*. She didn't wait. She inserted her desperate faith and withdrew from that divine pool of supernatural honey.

What she did was so uncommon that it actually startled Him. *"Who touched me? Someone touched me! I felt the pull! Someone took a sip"* (Luke 8:45).

The guys with him brushed it off, saying, *"the crowd is all over you! Everyone is touching you Lord"* (Luke 8:45).

But this was different. She pressed in so deep, she basically demanded the *favour* to be deposited into her body! The *good* here was her urgent faith, not necessarily her lack of observance in customary religious protocols (Luke 8:48).

Jesus, you are our source!
You are our help!
You are our healer!
YOU are the favour we need!

In The Pages

How many things in your life are under your limited management? When is the last time you genuinely cried out to Him for help? Who else can you remember from scripture who had this same desperation?

The Just Will Wear It

July 13
Proverbs 13

"Good people leave an inheritance to their grandchildren, but the sinner's wealth passes to the godly." Proverbs 13:22, NLT

"A good life gets passed on to the grandchildren; ill-gotten wealth ends up with good people." Proverbs 13:22, MSG

If you want the real scoop on what Wisdom says will become of the *sinner's* stuff, read these words from Job:

"This is the portion of a wicked man from God, and the inheritance which tyrants receive from the Almighty. Though his sons are many, they are destined for the sword; and his descendants will not be satisfied with bread. His survivors will be buried because of the plague, and their widows will not be able to weep. **Though he piles up silver like dust and prepares garments as plentiful as the clay, he may prepare it, but the just will wear it and the innocent will divide the silver.** *He has built his house like the spider's web, or as a hut, which the watchman has made. He lies down rich, but never again; he opens his eyes, and it is no longer. Terrors overtake him like a flood; a tempest steals him away in the night. The east wind carries him away, and he is gone, for it whirls him away from his place. For it will hurl at him without sparing; he will surely try to flee from its power. Men will clap their hands at him and will hiss him from his place"* (Job 27:13-23, NASB).

Brutal, huh? There is no "might," or "maybe," or "possibly," here. It's simple: when a person lives only to satisfy his own selfish desires, he's basically stockpiling for another's more righteous cause down the road!

It's a common theme. Here are a few examples of what I mean:

"He who increases his wealth by interest and usury gathers it for him who is gracious to the poor (Proverbs 28:8, NASB).

"For to a person who is good in His sight He has given wisdom and knowledge and joy, while to the sinner He has given the task of gathering and collecting so that he may give to one who is good in God's sight (Ecclesiastes 2:26, NASB).

"He may prepare it, but the just will wear it" (Job 27:17, NASB).

Catchy, ain't it?

On the other side of the coin, the men and women who walk with God will be able to pass everything they've earned down to their children and their children's children. Wisdom sees this as the continuation of the blessing! Although this includes wealth and possessions, it's not limited to just tangibles.

This also includes their knowledge of God, their faith, and their understanding of the works of the Lord. It may even include the "passing of mantles" (1 Kings 19:19).

Patti and I have spent most of our adult lives giving away our "stuff," rather than collecting material possessions and building a portfolio. We've attempted to believe the Lord's words,

"But seek first His kingdom and His righteousness, and all these things will be added to you" (Matthew 6:33, NASB).

What we have been able to pass on to our children and our grandchildren is the knowledge of the tangible presence of the Lord. Not just the ancient stories of what HE has done, but to actually show them the works of the Holy Spirit . . . today!

So when it comes to your inheritance, there will always be some stuff to sort through. Some of it will be special to you. Most of it is salvage-worthy. But the real goods, the eternal blessings, will come from the memories of what you've experienced because your elders plowed through the fields of faith!

That my friend is the real "cash" of the Kingdom!

In The Pages

Read Matthew 6:19-21. What kind of inheritance do you want to pass on to your grandchildren? Are they primarily tangibles or spiritual? What is your plan to acquire those goods in order to pass them on to those behind you?

Rod of Pride

July 14
Proverbs 14

"A fool's talk brings a rod to his back, but the lips of the wise protect them." Proverbs 14:3, NIV

"In the mouth of a fool is a rod of pride, but the lips of the wise will preserve them." Proverbs 14:3, NKJV

What an interesting play of words! The sheer poetry! You kind of need to think about what Solomon is saying here in order to really grasp it. He's saying more than one thing.

We assume the *"rod to his back"* in the NIV translation is just the normal, routine ass whipping a fool needs in order to shut his mouth when out of line. A most welcomed thought, but not quite the full essence of what Wisdom is saying here.

Usually when we think of the word *"rod,"* especially in Proverbs, we think of the wooden instrument or branch used to punish, discipline, or fight with (Proverbs 10:13, 13:24, 22:15, 23:13-14, 26:3, 29:15), or the stick, board, paddle, or plank that you're about to get pummeled with.

In today's verse, however, the Hebrew uses a different word for *rod*. The word is **chôṭer** (pronounced *kho´-ter*) meaning, *"twig."* A Hebrew reading this Proverb would have made a slightly different connection more in line with the NKJV version.

The *"rod* (or twig) *of pride"* grows outwardly because of a root that exists in the *fool's* heart. In other words, the root determines the manifestation, because they are tied together.

So in looking at the NKJV translation, we see that what comes out of the *mouth of a fool* sounds and computes as *pride*, because *pride* is deeply rooted in the heart. It's just a normal manifestation of that *"pride-full"* root.

Here's another thought that would have been common understanding back then. I'm obviously speaking in our contemporary terms, but you'll get the idea. The manifestation of *pride* carries such odious properties, there's only one way to shut down a person's foolish display of pride:

EXTERNAL PRESSURE!

In the package (inside of the pressure that pride creates), Wisdom spawns the inclination to justly render action that will bring a due correction to the fool. In other words, when a fool starts spouting off prideful rhetoric, mercifully there will usually be someone more seasoned with wisdom who will shut them down or bring the appropriate correction.

Some circles call that: FEEDBACK.

Yep, that's usually what happens. And don't we just love it when prideful arrogance finally gets put in its place?

NOTHING is further from the character of Christ than PRIDE.

NOTHING!

In The Pages

So the second part of today's Proverb teaches you what? How well do you tolerate the insolence in others? What is most bothersome to you? What they say, or how they say it?

Tapped In

July 15
Proverbs 15

"The Lord is far from the wicked, but he hears the prayer of the righteous." Proverbs 15:29, NRSV

Sometimes I get the feeling that Solomon, and all the other wisdom writers who contributed to our Holy writ, had just as much difficulty grasping the omnipresence of a good God as we do. If He's really present everywhere, all the time, why doesn't He communicate with us more readily? I mean, we've got some serious issues here, and we could all use some help getting this life crap figured out!

Today's Proverb says, *"He hears the prayer of the righteous."* Awesome! The word for *"hears"* is **shâma'** (pronounced *shaw-mah'*), which means, *"to hear intelligently."* God is paying attention. He knows our requests.

I think where we get our knickers in a twist is that we're not used to "quiet," and we expect a more "timely" response to our petitions. I mean we've got stuff to do, right?

We start to ask ourselves, does He even hear my prayers? The short answer is: YES. Is He obligated to respond? I'm okay with saying "yes" to that too, but He answers in *His* timing, not ours, and in *His* way, not ours.

Just because God doesn't respond today, doesn't mean He isn't responding. I personally believe that God is managing thousands, maybe millions, of providential puzzles on a constant basis. Yep, including yours.

So yes, He hears our prayers!

The first part of today's verse, however, implies that if you're a *wicked* person, God is so far from you that He does not hear your prayers. If you're wicked, you're S.O.L! This is sort of what David was talking about when he said,

"You have also made my enemies turn their backs to me, and I destroyed those who hated me. They cried for help, but there was none to save, even to the Lord, but He did not answer them. Then I beat them fine as the dust before the wind; I emptied them out as the mire of the streets" (Psalms 18:40-42, NASB).

At times, David displayed some serious swagger and confidence in his relationship with the Lord! He's basically saying,

> *"If you mess with me, then you've picked a fight with my Dad, and He is going to wear your ass out!"*

Quite honestly, we need some of that! If we had this kind of confidence in our own relationships with the Lord, we'd be a lot less prone to fear and the religion that plague us.

But which *wicked* person did Jesus ever stiff-arm or turn his back on?

Please, just hear me out before you blow a gasket. *"The Lord is far from the wicked."* What could that possibly mean?

I've been wicked before. You've been wicked before (probably, maybe). How far was God from you when you called for Him? How long did it take for Him to answer your prayers when you realized you needed Him and were ready to make a change?

Quite frankly, I've never found God to be far from me. Even when I was a disgusting mess, He never refused me.

It's when we make the "turn" that we realize we've always been in His presence. His light holds all darkness! He is not deterred by our weaknesses or foul behaviors.

I'm not calling David or Solomon liars, but Jesus (who was God with skin) showed us that the wicked and sinners were welcome and loved regardless of their crap! He is THE GOOD NEWS!

Besides, David often experienced the love and mercy of God:

*"The Lord is near **to all who call upon Him**, to **all who call upon Him in truth**. He will fulfill the desire of those who fear Him; He will also hear their cry and will save them"* (Psalms 145:18-19, NASB).

The Holy Spirit satisfies the thirsty heart and is drawn to those who think they don't deserve His goodness. Can we be truly thankful for God's ability to see through our crap and hear our pleas?

In The Pages

Read Hebrews 4:8-10. What all is included in this promise? How much confidence do you have in that? When is the last time you sat in real confidence that God knows what is happening in your life?

Creating Breaches

July 16
Proverbs 16

"Better a patient man than a warrior, a man who controls his temper than one who takes a city." Proverbs 16:32, NIV

"He who is slow to anger is better than the mighty, and he who rules his spirit, than he who captures a city." Proverbs 16:32, NASB

"Moderation is better than muscle, self-control better than political power." Proverbs 16:32, MSG

"Like a city that is broken into and without walls is a man who has no control over his spirit." Proverbs 25:28, NASB

What I envision here is the horrible damage done by a breach. You've heard the terms "breach of contract," "breach of confidentiality," and "breach of peace." What we're talking about here today is the "breach of *character*." The contravention of moral character and the failure of two people to reach a spiritual agreement bring so much destruction, it seems almost beyond repair.

It can happen suddenly, in a moment of selfishness, from the upper levels of leadership down to the forces of erosion underneath. And once that breach forms, a flooding of destruction is soon to follow. I've been around ministry and church a long time, and I've seen it happen more times than I care to remember.

There are several different words for *"anger"* in the Hebrew language. The one used today is **aph** (pronounced *af*), which means *"the nose or nostril."*

Today's Proverb describes the *patient* person who, though extremely pissed about something, is breathing through his nose (probably very fervently) in order to control themselves and keep from going ape-shit in a fit of rage. Clearly, this person understands the repercussions of relenting and giving in to his natural urge to blow up something.

This kind of individual is controlled enough to maintain composure and assess questions like: *"what are the terms here?" "What has been previously agreed upon",* and *"how do we best address this issue so everyone wins?"*

"Ruling the spirit," means that we don't give in to what our impulses really want to do in those moments. Instead, real strength chooses to manifest legitimate concern for those under and around us, and we try to come up with a better alternative than waging war.

Peterson's version calls it *moderation*. Thinking and acting in honorable terms. Something more than shoddy lip service.

Sadly, a lot of changes in ministry happen because of the selfish-ambition of a single man, his impatience, and an unwillingness to work out honorable terms of agreement where everyone wins.

Have you ever visited a small town and wondered why there were four different congregations, all deriving from the same denomination? People quit talking, start swinging, and go their separate ways. That's when the breach appears, the wall falls, and the floods of destruction begin to rise.

"For where jealousy and selfish ambition exist, there is disorder and every evil thing" (James 3:16, NASB).

Wow! What a telling verse.

In The Pages

How do you feel after you lose your temper? Are you willing to say, "I was wrong?" Are you still angry about something that happened a year ago? Longer?

Buzzard Puke

July 17
Proverbs 17

"Even a fool, when he keeps silent, is considered wise; when he closes his lips, he is considered prudent." Proverbs 17:28, NASB

One of the most colorful personalities of my teenage years was my sixth grade P.E. instructor, Coach Shepherd. He also taught me Texas History in seventh grade, was my Jr. High football and basketball coach, and also my Junior Varsity and Varsity basketball coach.

This cat was old school! Evidently, Marcus Shepherd was quite the stud during his college years. He had worked in the education system most of his adult life. I caught him towards the end of his career.

By the time I made the Varsity basketball team, I was the only white kid on the team. Yip, I looked like a six-foot-five inch, 170 pound white bean in high tops. Needless to say, I stood out on the court.

Coach and I had a long history together. I'm still somewhat famous (40 years later), for Coach yelling at me in the gym,

> *"Paschall, I'm gonna make you run until your breath smells like buzzard puke!"*

Welcome to my adolescent nightmare. Coach Shepherd was an equal mix of General George Patton, and Red Foxx. Yeah, it sucked back to be in 6th grade back then. Coach could get crotchety.

In Coach Shepherd's seventh-grade history class, we were required to keep a notebook of Proverbs that he would write up on the chalkboard each day when we walked into his room. He called it **Food For Thought**. It didn't take but two minutes to copy down what was up there, but apparently that was too much work for "yours truly."

I wasn't very consistent in remembering to do it, even though a completed notebook meant a major help to your grades in that class. Kind of gives you an idea about my grades in Junior High.

One day the Proverb written on Coach Shepherd's board read,

> *"Even a fool, when he holdeth his peace, is counted wise: and he that shutteth his lips is esteemed a man of understanding."*

He gave us five minutes to copy it down. Then Coach went on some rant about how kids need to learn how to be quiet in order to process information.

"You can't learn by flappin' yo jaws all the time!" During his exposition, I was in the back of the room, mumbling under my breath about how stupid this whole **Food For Thought** thing was and causing a bit of a commotion.

Suddenly I heard, *"Paschall!"* Oh frik, here it comes. *"I can't see you back there."* If only I had taken heed of today's Proverb.

"I can't see you either," I replied. The room absolutely exploded in laughter. The chick I was trying to impress next to me threw both hands over her mouth, like I just signed my death warrant.

Coach said nothing. He didn't smile. He got up, walked to the back of the room, grabbed the back of my chair, and dragged me all the way to the front of the room, where he parked me beside his desk. Yeah, that was my new seat assignment for the rest of the year. And he gave me his own personalized interpretation of the verse.

"Paschall, it's better to let people wonder if you're a fool, than to open your mouth and prove it in front of everyone."

Must have been the buzzard puke.

In The Pages

"Why did I ever open my mouth?" How many times have you said this to yourself? What was the circumstance? Were there consequences? Was it a matter of poor choice of words, or bad timing? Can you be quiet when you need to be quiet?

Send a note of thanks to a teacher today. They might have the most valuable, yet unappreciated job on the planet! Teachers do what they do for some other reason than money. Be sure to say "Thank You!" —MDP 2018

Rock Me, Baby

July 18
Proverbs 18

"The one who finds a wife finds what is enjoyable, and receives a pleasurable gift from the Lord." Proverbs 18:22, NET

Amen, brother. AMEN!

I had a good talk with my wife before writing today's devotional. We discussed this verse in length. I think we're both in agreement that both men and women need a greater understanding of this scripture. Let's look at the text.

Most translations say, *"and obtains favor from the Lord"*, versus *"receives a pleasurable gift from the Lord"*, which I suspect translators were not as comfortable with. Honestly, I have an easier time believing that my wife is pleasure to me, rather than a magic pill that gives me favor.

Since *favor* is tied to God's purpose, this translation implies that she helps me get stuff done. True enough, but in the Hebrew, it's clear that *she* is the gift that brings me raw and real pleasure, and God is totally good with that!

So I asked Patti a simple question. "If a newly married young woman was sitting on your couch asking you how to pleasure her man, what would you say?" Her response was genius. *"It is sensual, but not always sexual. There are lots of ways to bring pleasure, and they're all legitimate."* Perfect!

"Like what?" I asked. *"She can keep herself fit, she can steward the beauty she has, she can know what moves his heart, she can communicate and build sexual expectations verbally, she can avail herself to his sensual and sexual desires with regular attention to details."* God, I love this woman!

The concern Patti and I both have is that life brings so many interruptions, stressful situations, complications, and trials, that the attention to sensual details are challenged on a regular basis. Couples have to fight like hell to remain in-tune together!

Compared to 100 years ago, life has gotten so much more complicated, not less. So we have to pay more attention to the details of good marital sensuality. The numbers are not pretty in regards to marriages staying healthy. We have to do a better job of taking care of the most important thing in our lives.

Men, do you realize that she is a "gift" to you? Do you romance her, pursue her, dig into her heart, explore her spirit, rejoice in her beauty, and touch her with youthful wonder and amazement? She needs that!

It doesn't matter how long you have been together. If you'll cultivate love and romance her passions . . . well, the rewards are substantial.

And ladies, do you love yourself enough to recognize what your husband loves about you? Do you recognize his needs and nurture respect for him, especially when he's failed or blown it? He doesn't need another mother. He needs a passionate woman who walks with God to tend to his spirit.

Yeah baby, you're a special gift—one of a kind! Make sure you both know it!

In The Pages

Singles: Read, learn, and prepare in faith.

Husbands: How much energy are you expending in cultivating passion and romance? What kind of turn-on are you for her? You need to think about it.

Wives: When is the last time you planned an evening of romance that was all about his pleasure? Most men will lose their minds at the thought of it!

Passionate Plea

July 19
Proverbs 19

"Stop listening to instruction, my son, and you will stray from the words of knowledge." Proverbs 19:27, NIV

This verse did it for me today, for several different reasons. This is the only place we read the words *"my son"* between Proverbs 7:1 and 23:15. That's a huge gap!

Here, in this one verse, Solomon speaks passionately from the heart. Not to say that the rest of Proverbs wasn't, but it's so very obvious here. He really wants his kid to get this.

We should all appreciate a voice of Wisdom that has the weight of experience on it. Solomon isn't peddling hypothetical snake oil here.

It kind of makes you wonder, doesn't it? Solomon was indeed wise, but he was also a man. He'd been through some crap and made some gross mistakes (1 Kings 11:6). Life hadn't been a sterile laboratory for him. And honestly, Jesus is the only One who did it all right. We are all better off learning from the strengths AND weaknesses in man.

"But prove yourselves doers of the word, and not merely hearers who delude themselves. For if anyone is a hearer of the word and not a doer, he is like a man who looks at his natural face in a mirror; for once he has looked at himself and gone away, he has immediately forgotten what kind of person he was" (James 1:22-24, NASB).

This is exactly what Solomon is talking about. The first Sr. Pastor of Jerusalem is giving a heart-felt pitch to his sheep.

If you think this instruction by James is about trying harder to keep all the rules, you'd be putting severe restrictions on such a rich deposit. The Pastor wanted his people to stay versed and in touch with who they really were.

It wasn't about getting more rules inside of them. James had a great desire for the sheep to grow in their understanding and live fully in the abundance and expanse of what Jesus had done for them. It wasn't theory.

The instruction was to acknowledge the truth (word & Spirit), live the truth, and be the truth! To *stop listening* would put them all at risk, and *straying* brought serious challenges to the sheep.

BTW, you're more than halfway through the year now. Kudos for establishing some disciplines in your life: scripture reading, devotions, prayer, and journaling. Giving yourself some time and space each day to hear from the Holy Spirit is legit! It is a "choice" option for allowing God to remind you of who you really are!

It's rough out there, and most of the world has an opinion of what and where we should be investing ourselves. We need to be reminded daily: this is who I am, this is what I care about, this is what I'm trying to accomplish, and the Words of life (logos and Ghost) are what really give me life! You get my drift?

Dude, fight for your time with Jesus! Don't wimp out! Deny your impulses to spin in activity and succumb to every urgent cry of the now. Take a dip in God's spa, and learn to chill in it. It is a discipline that strengthens us and prepares us to be *"effectual doers"* (James 1:25). It's extremely important to realize these things!

In The Pages

So, how consistent have you become in your spiritual disciplines? What is your biggest battle with getting "down-time" with the Lord? Early on, I had to make a daily appointment and set an alarm to develop consistency. Where and how do you improve and strengthen your desire for commitment?

Backstabbers

July 20
Proverbs 20

"He who goes about as a slanderer reveals secrets, therefore do not associate with a gossip." Proverbs 20:19, NASB

BACKSTABBERS
(*What they do*)
(*They smile in your face*)
All the time they want to take your place
The backstabbers (*backstabbers*)
*Leon Huff, Gene McFadden, John Whitehead © Warner/Chappell Music, Inc.
Used by permission.*

It brings me no pleasure to write this, but in all my years of ministry experience, more times that I care to admit, I've seen seriously anointed men (not to be confused with managers of ministry or church—it's not always the same thing) be discredited from an opportunity of service because of slander. I mean, dead in the water before they even had a chance to bring real help, real relief, and spiritual gifts that would support the cause of Kingdom.

Slander is alive and well out there, and it does its damage. I could get really passionate about this, so I'll just leave it right here before I go off on a rant.

We picture people sitting around, drinking coffee and ripping to shreds everyone around them with poisoned words and daggered opinions. Truth be known, boredom probably does play a role. But it goes much deeper than that, and the relational cancer involved is a serious problem.

"A perverse man spreads strife, and a slanderer separates intimate friends"
(Proverbs 16:28, NASB).

Jesus! This is terrible! It's slightly nauseating to even mention it.

We can understand strife and separation, right? It's more than someone just creating doubt and suspicion. It's much darker and ultimately deadly. This is wicked business, and sadly, it is much too common in our spiritual culture.

"Slander" is a demonic presence that seeks to nullify the witness of the Holy Spirit among anointed men and women who are called to serve the Lord in team and unity. I see it surface whenever ministry is treated like a business and people are considered the currency of the trade.

If all you're getting is lip service when it comes to the parameters of honor, respect, submission, and the flow of spiritual authority, you can expect the full expression of self-seeking and get-ahead tactics.

None of those things are appropriate for any true spiritual climate.

Yeah, *slander* will backstab in a heartbeat. In fact, that is exactly what it does. It doesn't care about the potential damages. It has no respect for relationship or honor. It just wants to keep everything under its control and management

Paul groups the guilty with the *"haters of God"* (Romans 1:30). Ok, maybe I ranted . . . just a little bit.

In The Pages

Have you ever had your credibility sliced before you even showed up? What does it feel like to know you're being measured on the front end of a relationship? Why do you think "ministry" people are ruthlessly prone to gossip and slander?

Love Does

July 21
Proverbs 21

"The one who shuts his ears to the cry of the poor, he too will cry out and will not be answered." Proverbs 21:13, NET

It happens every time I come across one of these passages dealing with the poor. I actually grimace at the forthright brutality of Wisdom's simple bluntness. Every verse in Proverbs that deals with poverty makes it very clear that God has zero tolerance for us overlooking the needs of the poor. There is no wiggle room. Today's proverb is no exception.

I want to redirect you to a letter the Apostle John wrote to encourage the adolescent church. Some commentaries date the letter to around 100 A.D., so the church had seen some stuff, been through some disappointment, and had its share of false teachers and fabricators of theological cocktails. There was a variety of doctrine being offered at this time, and sometimes you just need good ole dad to weigh in and dissolve the confusion. So the Apostle John did just that... BIG time!

"By this the children of God and the children of the devil are obvious: anyone who does not practice righteousness is not of God, nor the one who does not love his brother. For this is the message which you have heard from the beginning, that we should love one another; not as Cain, who was of the evil one and slew his brother. And for what reason did he slay him? Because his deeds were evil, and his brother's were righteous. Do not be surprised, brethren, if the world hates you. We know that we have passed out of death into life, because we love the brethren. He who does not love abides in death. Everyone who hates his brother is a murderer; and you know that no murderer has eternal life abiding in him. We know love by this that He laid down His life for us; and we ought to lay down our lives for the brethren. ***But whoever has the world's goods, and sees his brother in need and closes his heart against him, how does the love of God abide in him?*** *Little*

children, let us not love with word or with tongue, but in deed and truth"* (1 John 3:10-18, NASB).

Basically, this is an overview by the Apostle on how we Christians are supposed to love. His words, influenced by the Lord, are a smack in the face.

Verse 17 lands like a ton of bricks. It presses on us. It's not about guilt! It's about our responsibility to think of needs beyond our own.

Look, when you're munching on your favorite pizza and that commercial with the little kid with the doe eyes, dirty face, and bloated belly comes on, that's not the time to liquidate your stock portfolio in order to write a big check to charity. But what are we doing on a consistent basis to address the needs of the impoverished around us?

Love says we must do something. Wisdom agrees.

In The Pages

How do we close our ears to the cries of the poor? Are there impoverished people who live in your community? Who is reaching out to them with help?

Mind and Lips

July 22
Proverbs 22

"Incline your ear and hear the words of the wise, and apply your mind to my knowledge; for it will be pleasant if you keep them within you, that they may be ready on your lips. So that your trust may be in the Lord, I have taught you today, even you. Have I not written to you excellent things of counsels and knowledge, to make you know the certainty of the words of truth that you may correctly answer him who sent you?" Proverbs 22:17-21, NASB

These are Lady Wisdom's introductory thoughts, immediately preceding the "30 Wise Sayings of the Ancients" (Proverbs 22:22-24:34). This is Wisdom telling us why it's important to get truth inside of us.

In more modern terms, we're talking about the basic tenants of discipleship. That means we build relationships and stick with them long enough to establish basic growth patterns of "Spirit"uality that form habits and disciplines for Word consumption. We also give honest feedback, which promotes character development. It's a tedious process that requires quite a bit of patience on both ends of the relationship.

Wisdom employs the learner (the one being discipled) to open himself up enough to let this tried and true process take effect, to "tuck-up-under" in a trusting relationship, and let the Word saturate. Store the Word deep inside of yourself and it will always be readily available to you, even when an unexpected situation demands an unprepared response.

I can't help but think about the strong men and women in scripture who stood in these incredibly pressured situations, yet words of wise counsel and seasoned fortitude bubbled forth in abundance. People like Esther, Daniel, Joseph, and Solomon had all been trained, schooled, and embraced the disciplines of ingesting truth.

When a need arose, the Spirit anointed, and the internal possession of their learning became obvious. Jesus discussed this same process with a few of His disciples.

Peter, James, Andrew, and John were quizzing Him one day about reading the signs of the future. Jesus warned them,

"For nation will rise up against nation, and kingdom against kingdom; there will be earthquakes in various places; there will also be famines. These things are merely the beginning of birth pangs. But be on your guard; for they will deliver you to the courts, and you will be flogged in the synagogues, and you will stand before governors and kings for My sake, as a testimony to them. The gospel must first be preached to all the nations" (Mark 13:8-10, NASB).

Then He added,

"When they arrest you and hand you over, do not worry beforehand about what you are to say, but say whatever is given you in that hour; for it is not you who speak, but it is the Holy Spirit" (Mark 13:11, NASB).

In short, it would be impossible to prepare a discourse for these types of situations. But because of all of the truth and wisdom already downloaded, the Holy Spirit draws on those wells of Wisdom and brings to *mind* and *lips* the proper answers! This is a legit promise, even for today!

In The Pages

How have you seen the truth of today's Proverb play out in your own life? When is the last time you memorized scripture? Is that difficult for you? Why?

You Gotta Get Your Mind Right!

July 23
Proverbs 23

"My son, if your heart is wise, then my heart will be glad; my inmost being will rejoice when your lips speak what is right." Proverbs 23:15-16, NIV

My grandchildren love tickle games almost as much as I love tickling them. We play this one game where I count each of their ribs, and they have to try not to smile during the process. It's impossible.

I always tell them, "You gotta get your mind right." Immediately, they go stone-faced in preparation, but it's to no avail. The eruption of laughter is inevitable.

Not too long ago, they were both in the pool, bobbing like corks with their life jackets on, begging for yours truly to do a cannonball from the ledge. I consented, of course.

But right before I jumped, I asked them if they were ready. In unison, they said, *"Yeah...but Ba* [that's what they call me... "Ba"], *you gotta get your mind right!"* They're four years old! They absorb everything.

It is an extremely rewarding moment when you realize your kids are actually putting to use the life skills you've taught them. In the early years, just them mimicking you feels good.

These little people who look like you, are now acting like you as well. As they grow up, it absolutely wrecks you to see them go after life with grace, wisdom, and honor. It's validation that the stuff you taught them got deep into their hearts. You begin to see all of your labor to build a strong foundation finally paying off.

The Holy Spirit has even expanded on their gifts and skills, and they've moved beyond you. They are following another voice, the voice of the One who has much more influence and stroke with their value systems. It's the best reward I could ever hope for.

"Then my heart will be glad; my inmost being will rejoice..." I know what he means.

I don't remember reading anywhere in the Gospels where Jesus told someone they couldn't follow Him. Usually, He'd invite someone to follow Him and they would either choose other priorities, or else make a grandiose show of their willingness to follow, without realizing what they were actually committing themselves to (Luke 9:57-62).

In short, they hadn't gotten their mind (or their heart) right.

When we decide to go the distance, I mean *really* go the distance with the Lord; it fills His heart with that same joy we feel when we see growth and maturity in those we're raising up. Jesus was spot-on when He said,

> *"No one, after putting his hand to the plow and looking back, is fit for the kingdom of God"* (Luke 9:62, NASB).

You can't be *"sort of"* committed to plowing. You can't be *"sort of"* committed to harvesting. We have to be fully vested in a process that we know will produce fruit in due time.

It's go big or go home!

The same is true for Wisdom. It requires a consistent commitment to Wisdom's character. Don't judge the results today. Plow deep. Wait. You'll see fruit soon enough.

Come on, you gotta get your mind right!

In The Pages

Remember, one of the goals is for you to read through all of Proverbs twelve times in one year. Are you reading the entire chapter daily? How much new info have you become aware of in this process?

Cold-cocked

July 24
Proverbs 24

"If you are slack in the day of distress, your strength is limited." Proverbs 24:10, NASB

I remember the birth of our third grandchild like it was yesterday. My youngest daughter knows how to *"git-r-done."*

Hospital by 7:30am, water broken, Pitocin drip by 8:30am, epidural at 9:00am, pushing by 12:15pm, crying baby 15 minutes later. Simple, right?

The girl did the same thing with twins on her first go-round. It was like clockwork! So we did the traditional thing—standing at the thick glass, watching the nursery aids give the kid his first bath.

All fingers and toes were in place, along with a nice head of dark hair to compliment that beautifully smooth skin. Most newborns look like miniature old people. Our guy was a beauty.

So it was high fives all around, lots of tears, and hugs among the family. God surely outdid himself this time. It was the perfect entrance for our new little prince. Time to ice the champagne and celebrate.

Until she showed up.

"We hear a clicking noise in his heart," she said.

She was uncertain, jittery and uncomfortable, and we all knew it.

"We want to keep him in the nursery and have him checked out by one of the specialists. It could be nothing, or it could be a problem. We need to find out."

Every molecule of festive air was sucked out of that room in about 10 seconds.

A potential heart issue wasn't on anyone's radar. *Fear* barged in like it owned the joint! As quickly as our hearts had leapt when we heard Lewis's first cry declare his place in this world, they sank in that one, sobering moment.

I took my daughter's trembling hand as she sobbed into her husband's chest. It was almost too much to bear.

All I had, all any of us had was, "we need to pray!"

I choked something out, a few words—not sure what, but it didn't really matter. We just needed Him to know that we needed Him.

It wasn't bold or grandiose. Honestly, it was nothing more than the collective groan of our utter distress and fear.

Our story has a happy ending. No issues for our little man. He lives a normal existence. But that little incident scared the hell into us. It really made me think about today's scripture.

My family is full of strong, faith-filled warriors, but *fear* absolutely cold-cocked us in that moment! Fortunately, we recovered just enough to press into Him... fear and all! In hindsight, maybe we should all consider the possibility that our prayers for those who can't pray for themselves might be one of the best things we can do for each other!

People get stuck in their pain, stuck in their fear, and they shut down in their paralyzed faith. I see this differently than I used to. Religious piousness would make recited prayers or the Bible a "quick fix" to our every problem.

It's not the ritual we need, but the connection with Him! If it's via prayer, so be it!

So here is the lesson: flex your strength, or lean on someone else's for that matter! But do something. Prayer is always a viable option!

In The Pages

When is the last time you were so afraid that you couldn't respond to the situation at hand? How did you bust loose into action?

Miss Daisy's Floaters

July 25
Proverbs 25

"Like the cold of snow in time of harvest is a faithful messenger to those who send him, for he refreshes the soul of his masters." Proverbs 25:13, NKJV

The last parsonage my family and I lived in was sandwiched between the church I pastored and an elderly widow who didn't attend our church. Directly across the street lived the widow's sister-in-law, an old maid.

Being the young pastor I was, with my red cape glistening and blue tights rippled, I mowed both of their yards every time I did my own. My neighbor next door had a very small yard, done in 20 minutes easy. Across the street, on the other hand, was a small, un-kept jungle, which required skill, agility, a strong stomach (you'll understand why later) and zero fear of burrowed varmints or critters of any kind. What I'm about to share with you happened every time I mowed Miss Daisy's yard.

She had to be in her upper '70s. You could tell that at one time she had been a very well manicured lady. But time, and a crippling stroke, had done a real number on her.

It took almost an hour and a half for me to mow her yard. I would be soaked through with sweat, and then I'd see her coming. She'd bring this huge, faded Slurpee cup, wrapped in tin foil, which had been through one too many cycles in the dishwasher. That was always my cue to start praying.

So she'd walk sideways, dragging one leg, splashing water on herself in the process. The cup was too big to grab with her good hand, so she'd cradle it between her good arm and her curled wrist.

Then, you'd notice that her hair had been combed, and her lipstick was freshly applied. I'd turn the mower off and take the cup from her gratefully.

It was usually water and about eight freezer burned ice cubes. But the real suspense was in trying to figure out which casserole, or leftover, that same tin foil had covered the night before. There were always floaters.

Miss Daisy liked watching a man drink, so I'd be obliged to chug all 72 ounces, swallow the floaters, and thank the Lord for her beautiful heart and concern for my well being! In all honestly, she was pure refreshment!

Today, Wisdom reminds us how exhilarating it is to actually have someone in your life you can count on. Someone you can trust, confide in, and know they've got your back, no matter what. Whether it's family or friends, it settles us and makes our journeys so much richer.

"Like the cold of snow in the time of harvest," is not about an out-of-season snowfall. Many times in the ancient Middle East, fresh winter snow was gathered and kept in caves. That snow could be sold and purchased, even as late as the fall harvest.

Imagine a hot and sweaty laborer who is offered a drink, cooled by that snow. Yes, by this time there were probably some floaters in the mix, but that kind of refreshment had to be an encouragement to finish their job strong! It's really something to be thankful for!

In The Pages

Besides the Lord, who helps supply you with generous doses of refreshment? Do you reciprocate or just take from them? What would really refresh them in return?

Madman at the Gate

July 26
Proverbs 26

"Like a madman who throws firebrands, arrows, and death, is the man who deceives his neighbor, and says, "I was only joking!" Proverbs 26:18-19, NKJV

He saw the smoke long before he could see the problem. For every minute his horse galloped, the knot in his stomach grew stronger and clinched tighter. David was prophetic enough to know that once he got over the next hill, he would be able to see home, and what he dreaded most (1 Samuel 30).

The town of Ziklag had been a gift to David from Achish, Lord of the Philistines. It had been a much-needed refuge from that maniac who loved him, yet wanted to kill him. It had been a trying couple of days. The

Philistine military staff did not trust David at all. David had been wondering about that all day. A long day on a horse lets a man do a lot of thinking.

Sometimes looking backwards and reconstructing the chain of events over a period of time can be the best teacher of wisdom. We know today's text was spoken by Solomon. Could it be that the King not only played back the tapes from his own life, but also the reruns from his Dad's life?

David, his mentor, maybe his greatest example of what it means to live fully alive, had some experiences to learn from—some good, some bad and some very bad. Solomon was very good at taking time to absorb the facts and then draw conclusions.

As hard as it was to swallow, David had a few issues with deception. All men who manifest sin have problems with deception (sorry, I don't have time to develop that thought here), and Solomon's personal hero was no exception.

In today's Proverb, the *"deception,"* whether innocent or intentional, creates a chain reaction resulting in eventual damage. You already know what we're talking about here is true in theory and reality.

Days, months, and possibly years later, when David thought back to the Ziklag massacre—the women and children who were ravaged and carried off by the Amalekites and the torching of the city—I wonder if he ever regretted approaching the Philistine government for refuge? Earlier I mentioned the lack of trust from the Philistine military staff.

Could it have been because David's first contact with Achish was a sham?

David pretended to be insane, for Pete's sake (1 Samuel 21)! Sure, he had an explanation, but David frikk'n lied.

It's pretty clear that today's advice from Solomon is based on what he learned from this whole fiasco.

Before you form alliances that require some kind of deception on your part, you might want to consider that plain ole honor and integrity is the simple, yet purest way, to communicate.

If you can't be you, what's the frikk'n point?

In The Pages

Think about all of your relationships. Do people get the real you, or are you a chameleon depending on who you're with? What about your spiritual expressions? Are you living the truth of what you know and believe? If not, why all the deception?

Dead Roosters

July 27
Proverbs 27

"A constant dripping on a day of steady rain and a contentious woman are alike; He who would restrain her restrains the wind, and grasps oil with his right hand." Proverbs 27:15-16, NASB

Wisdom makes me laugh sometimes. It's so brutally raw, yet so simple and true. We have to chuckle at the realism.

We've all been around a *"contentious woman"* once or twice, and we know how exasperating it is to try to deal with her. We've seen her children roll their eyes and the look of embarrassment on her husband's face as she's ripping everyone around her to shreds. Yeah, it's funny to a point until the sad reality of it all sets in.

Movies always paint the pictures for me in more expressive tones. When I read about this woman, I generally think of Peach, a character in Larry McMurtry's *Lonesome Dove*. Our first introduction to her is just what you'd expect—angry, agitated, a size 18 shoved into a 12, marching and ready for combat.

As she barks her demands at the Sheriff, the rooster cradled in her arms starts to make a ruckus. In a fitful rage, Peach wrenches the poor rooster's neck as she growls, *"Guess that will teach him to peck me."* Message received! I'm pretty sure Deputy Roscoe, who witnessed the whole thing, might have peed himself... just a little.

There is wisdom in today's counsel. *Restraint* and *grasping* her doesn't fix the problem. In fact, that only tends to make matters worse.

There are five separate verses in Proverbs addressing the *contentious* female. Of those verses, the consensus is to get out of harm's way! Thanks a lot!

Shouldn't this gal get what she deserves? Or is it grace she needs?

Isn't that true for all of us? We got grace when we deserved punishment. We received mercy when we deserved death. We got forgiveness while judgment was in order.

Somewhere in these devotionals, I've already expressed my heart for this hurting woman's healing. I'm convinced she's manifesting because she's been wounded, abused, taken advantage of, or holds too many broken promises. So now, it's just easier for her to screech until she gets what she wants.

It's just another bitter prison of isolation.

No one can get to her because the locks are on the inside. She holds all the keys to relationship and granted trust.

I'm a big believer in the soaking presence of the Holy Spirit. Peach, and everyone like her (men can be crabby bitches too), needs to be fully immersed in the fruit-filled sangria of God's restoration. A total filling and permeation of *love, gentleness, kindness, patience, goodness, peace* and *joy*, could change her forever!

She needs to hear another voice, the voice of her Heavenly Father, who tells her that *who* she is IS NOT determined by *what* has happened to her.

Crappy stuff happens in life, and it may not be anyone's premeditated fault. Without the Holy Spirit, little will ever change. More roosters needlessly die. The rain continues to drip. And honey, there is a better way to exist!

In the Pages

When people see you coming, do they expect a growl, or love? Is the desert or rooftop the only safe place when you are in the room? Is that the fragrance you want coming off of your life? What holds you in that prison of isolation?

Measuring Cow Piles

July 28
Proverbs 28

"A rich man may be wise in his own eyes, but a poor man who has discernment sees through him." Proverbs 28:11, NIV

I have to admit; I had a bit of a humorous moment this morning while thinking about this verse. The way I first read the passage was this: *"A rich man may be wise in his own eyes, but a poor man who has discernment will call "bullshit" on him every time."* I actually said, "whaaaat?" I had to look again to see how it was actually written. I chuckled a bit and thought it might be time to unplug from writing these devos for a couple of days.

The difference-maker here is the guy with *discernment*.

The trappings of the rich do not easily influence a person who is endowed with understanding and the ability to perceive certain circumstances. He can appreciate the finer things in life, but is not willing to compromise his own values, or depreciate himself, based on what someone else has. Anyway, this isn't really about *riches*.

This Proverb is about *character*. If a person is a snake, it doesn't really matter if he's rich or poor, a snake is a snake, and the *discerning* person will call *"bullshit"* every time!

The phrase *"sees through him"* is **châqar** (pronounced *khaw-kar'*) meaning, *"to penetrate, to examine intimately, to find out, or search (out)."* Now the radar antenna has gone up, Doppler has kicked in, and the MRI has produced its results. It's an ugly thing for those who hide behind their *riches* to find out that all the stuff they've acquired can't hide true *character*.

It's next to impossible to enter into the "rest" of powerlessness from a place of privilege and plenty. Most of Jesus' words to the rich came from a place of frustration. He never pointed at their possessions and said, *"You're rich, so . . . you suck!"* But He did challenge their dependence on wealth for wellbeing and security.

In the midst of a very intense discussion about what it meant to be a follower, He said, *"For what does it profit a man to gain the whole world, and forfeit his soul?"* (Mark 8:36, NASB). Again, the Lord isn't just railing against wealth. It's more about us getting our priorities straight.

If your priorities *are* straight, and you just happen to be blessed in the wealth department . . . AWESOME! But don't think for a second that you automatically have the kiss of heaven because you live in a gated community with a four-car garage and a vacation home in the wine country. That stuff isn't going to last forever and there is a final dance at the end of the prom.

All farmers know that seeds are for planting, not just acquiring.

The blessing of *discernment* is that each one of us can look beyond externals and arrange our priorities according to another set of values other than materials and wealth. Last time I checked, *riches* were not included as one of the *"fruits of the Spirit"* (Galatians 5:22-23).

These are the eternal fruits we want the *discerning* (rich or poor) to measure in us every time!

In The Pages

Can you discern a dishonest person when you get around one? What do you see that keys your insight? Are the rich more trust worthy? What about the less fortunate? How do you help a person who is shallow and unaware of his facades?

Man Pleasers

July 29
Proverbs 29

"The fear of man brings a snare, but he who trusts in the Lord will be exalted." Proverbs 29:25, NASB

"The fear of human opinion disables; trusting in God protects you from that." Proverbs 29:25, MSG

Okay, let's break this passage down and sort out the rich meat. The Hebrew word for "*man*" is **âdâm** (pronounced *aw-dawm´*), and it simply means *"a human being, an individual, or mankind in general."* So this isn't about fearing bad guys. It's about people in general.

On another note, the type of *"fea*r" mentioned here in today's passage refers to *insecurity* and anxiety. Peterson paints it clearly as *disabling* fear. Wisdom is giving us a big smack on our heads here!

It's a problem when God's people give more credence to the opinion and pressure of *others* than to what God might actually be saying.

This stuff is like biscuits and gravy at a redneck picnic. Quite honestly, I can't help myself. Others? Mike, who are these *"others"* you're referring to? Well, they could be just about anyone or anything. The *fear of man* and the *man-pleasing* spirit have pretty much taken over our culture.

Anything that requires genuine faith in the unseen spiritual realm puts you in a direct confrontation with the mainline church and the rest of the world. These systems are not dependent upon faith or the supernatural for their modes of operation. That probably sounds like I'm being ugly, but I don't mean to be.

In *The Pursuit of God*, A. W. Tozer says,

"... for the scribe tells us what he has read and the prophet tells us what he has seen. The distinctions are not an imaginary one. Between the scribe who has read and the prophet who has seen there is a difference as wide as the sea. We are today overrun with orthodox scribes, but the prophets, where are they? The hard voice of the scribe sounds over evangelicalism, but the Church waits for the tender voice of the saint who has penetrated the veil and gazed with inward eye upon the Wonder of God."[1]

Bluntly, the *fear of man* is a demonic controller.

It attempts to keep Spirit-infused men and women tied into knots of performance and endless doctrinal debates. That *"inward eye"* Tozer refers to, longs for much more than just being safe and fundamentally proper.

The *fear of man* will never allow you to color outside of the lines spiritually. It's too dangerous. Experience is always minimized to sterility in comparison to understanding.

Why does the *fear of man* take this strategy?

Because ideas are always up for debate and can easily be negotiated, manipulated, and altered. It's why we allow the pressure of public opinion to control us. We want approval and to belong. We fear being alone and exposed. So we just drink the Kool-Aid being served.

Sooner or later, we all have to face our *fear of man*. People who are committed to following the voice of God are always going to have a hard time pleasing everyone. Somewhere down the line, we have to choose. Wisdom declares, *"...he who trusts the Lord will be exalted!"*

In The Pages

Look at how you dress, what you drive, where you go to hang out, and your overall life projection. How much of that is influenced by peers and culture? Are you really you, or are you falsely living the image that you want others to appreciate and applaud? Are you living in the fullness of your spiritual desires, or just "fitting in" because it's familiar?

Simple Wisdom

July 30
Proverbs 30

"Four things on earth are small, yet they are exceedingly wise: the ants are a people without strength, yet they provide their food in the summer; the badgers are a people without power, yet they make their homes in the rocks; the locusts have no king, yet all of them march in rank; the lizard can be grasped in the hand, yet it is found in kings' palaces." Proverbs 30:24-28, NRSV

I don't know if this makes any sense to you or not, but I kind of see this in black and white... as in... black and white television. Little Timmy and Lassie are sitting on the front porch with dear old dad, who is educating Timmy on the importance of diligence and discipline. Even though his dog is actually smarter than he is, Timmy absorbs his father's wisdom and agrees to stay in school and not run off with the circus clowns.

Man! How many jams did Lassie get Little Timmy out of all those years? That kid needed serious help. The family would have been in serious trouble without that dog!

What Agur is saying here is simple, yet brilliant. Any young kid could really glean encouragement from today's text. Basically, wisdom is available to anyone who wants it. No life experience needed.

We can all benefit from the teachings of wisdom. If these small bugs and critters can operate in wisdom, so can each one of us. Those things didn't go to school. They didn't study or succumb to discipline to learn to find food and build shelter. They just exist and do what they are naturally inclined to do. It's a sobering lesson for all of us.

Wisdom is available to us in such a broad spectrum. It's not limited to decision-making. I think we "church folk" lock wisdom into a category. We have a tendency to seek counsel and call upon wisdom for the big stuff, the crucial directives for living. There is nothing wrong with that, but Agur reminds us that wisdom is also available in our everyday lives.

We don't need a direct download from heaven to operate wisely. We have brains to help us make good choices. Doing even the simplest things well is creating and providing opportunities for blessing and security in our lives. It doesn't always have to be mystical or majestic.

Paying your bills on time, treating people with respect, honoring your parents, showing your friends some love—these things don't require an encounter with deity. It doesn't hurt, of course, but it's not always necessary either.

If bugs, lizards, and varmints can figure it out, we probably can too, right? If not, we all need to find our own Lassie. She'll know what to do. "Here, girl!"

In The Pages

Which of those four critter groups is most fascinating to you? What can you learn by just watching them? What other lessons have you learned from nature? Have you ever applied anything to your life that you've learned from the animal kingdom?

Cleaning the House

July 31
Proverbs 31

"The heart of her husband trusts in her, and he will have no lack of gain. She does him good and not evil all the days of her life" Proverbs 31:11-12, NASB

"The heart of her husband safely trusts her; so he will have no lack of gain. She does him good and not evil all the days of her life." Proverbs 31:11-12, NKJV

The only time I ever saw my dad's dad in church was at his own funeral. I would visit my grandparents in Arkansas for three weeks during the summer and occasionally at Christmas or Thanksgiving.

My grandmother grew up Pentecostal, so church was a big deal to her. She didn't drive, so we'd load up in the green Nova, and Pa-paw would drive her into Pine Bluff to whatever Assembly of God church she was frequenting at the time.

I was usually envious of him because after dropping us off, he'd go to a nearby cafe and eat a second breakfast. Once church was over, we'd walk out to the car and find him parked under some shaded tree, smoking one of his freshly rolled cigarettes, or dippin' snuff and reading the paper. It never dawned on me that he worked 10-20 hours of overtime each week, and Sunday was his only real day of rest and free time.

The story of my grandfather's life is rough. He was driven from his home at age 13 because of a stepfather who made his life a personal hell. Regular whippings with a razor strap left marks that didn't easily wash away. He ended up just another street kid who never knew his real dad.

Life had not been too kind to my Pa-paw until he met my grandmother. Sometimes it takes awhile for a person to be free of all the demons of severe rejection. Even with five small children at home and a faithful, loving wife, home wasn't a place that brought him much peace. It wasn't until the kids were grown that my Pa-paw finally found his home to be the steady refuge he had needed for so long.

I've said a lot about my Pa-paw, but this devo is actually about my Ma-maw. Vera was a giant in faith. She had to be. The woman had raised five children by herself, had endured a husband who was prisoner to the bottle, and she still believed in God for the good, especially concerning her marriage.

All I ever witnessed was her crazy love for him, and I've often wondered what it took for my grandfather to finally see that the front porch lights were always on at home.

Maybe it was because she never left?

Nonetheless, the home fires were always burning, and he was always welcomed back. Vera served her man like a crazy woman and loved him until her very last breath, which was long after he had departed this earth.

"For the unbelieving husband is sanctified through his wife, and the unbelieving wife is sanctified through her believing husband; for otherwise your children are unclean, but now they are holy" (1 Corinthians 7:14, NASB).

Oh, the sanctifying power of love!

I saw today's Proverb lived out in my grandparents' marriage. Pa-paw's eventual trust of Vera's unconditional love *"saved"* (**sōzō**, which is pronounced *sode´-zo*; meaning, *"to deliver or protect—heal, preserve, do well, be (make) whole"*) his life. They weren't perfect, but functionally happy and in love.

The beneficial spillage for the rest of the family was indeed glorious and sweet!

In The Pages

Of the verses listed today, which one speaks to you the clearest? Why?

I've come to believe that the "visa versa" effect of 1 Corinthians 7:14 is just as important as the original intent! I doubt Paul could foresee how deep the spirit of religion would dig into the lives of the followers of Jesus. Too often Christians need to remember that God's love and light applies to everyone. We too need deliverance from ourselves. A mate or friend who isn't bound up in religion's trappings might be very good medicine for us. —MDP 2018

Brine

August 1
Proverbs 1

"Therefore they will eat from the fruit of their way, and they will be stuffed full of their own counsel." Proverbs 1:31, NET

Have you ever watched the television show, My Strange Addiction? America's fascination with reality television, and our voyeuristic appetites, continues to lead us down paths that go behind the scenes of some crazy (if not sickening) human element stories.

As I was channel-surfing one evening, I stopped on TLC long enough to hear some of the details of a young woman who eats sheetrock. Supposedly, she isn't the only one. Another guy eats glass. His everyday visits to the toilet must be a nightmare! Ouch!

Anyone who knows my wife knows that she goes weak in the knees when you bring out the salsa and chips. Most anything salty is like candy to her! When Patti was pregnant with our first child, I made many a trip to McDonalds in those wee hours for french fries. It was the salt.

A couple of months before she delivered our first daughter, we were visiting her parents. She spotted an unopened jar of Spanish olives in the refrigerator. "A few olives won't hurt," she thought. That's how it innocently started.

Against the veteran warnings of her mother, and the look of concern on her husband's face, Patti emptied the entire jar, and then she drank the juice! ALL of it.

You know how the story ends. The poor woman turned the color of her delicacy and puked her guts out. To this day, she maintains that it was worth it. Ick!

In the last 13 verses of Proverbs 1, Solomon leans into us with his now familiar style. Lady Wisdom speaks, beseeching us to hear her voice and know her heart for us. Those who will not listen will only have themselves to blame.

The NASB translation uses the word *"satiated."* In the Hebrew, it's **sâbêaʻ** (pronounced *saw-bay'-ah*), and it does mean *"to be filled, or to have* *enough,"* but it also implies that we eventually grow weary of what we are full of—an initial fullness that ends in discontentment.

If we read the rest of the chapter, it's easy to see how this is possible. In a nutshell, we do it to ourselves. Our refusal to heed Wisdom leaves us full and sloshing in our own brine.

Sooner or later, all that we've ingested will come gushing forth in our lives. Will it be a blessing to those around us, or do we need to stick our heads in the commode for proper disposal? Wisdom leaves that part for us to figure out.

In The Pages

Have you ever tasted the fruit of your own way? What have you learned in hindsight? What would you do differently now?

Here And Now

August 2
Proverbs 2

"For the upright will live in the land, and the blameless will remain in it; but the wicked will be cut off from the land, and the unfaithful will be torn from it." Proverbs 2:21-22, NIV

"It's the men who walk straight who will settle this land, the women with integrity who will last here. The corrupt will lose their lives; the dishonest will be gone for good." Proverbs 2:21-22, MSG

King Solomon, like every Israelite of that time, had a paradigm. Residing in the land that God gave them was evidence enough of His love and favor. And Solomon's father had shown that God was extremely dialed in to individual relationships with mankind.

But the nation as a whole was still managing life under Mosaic covenant. Getting to live in the land was dependent upon obedience and reverence towards the Law. Even here in today's text, it says, *blameless* and you stay, *wicked* and you're gone. There wasn't much gray. Everything was cut and dry, black and white, right and wrong, good and evil.

Take a moment and read Deuteronomy 28. It's a very telling chapter that pretty much confirms what Solomon is talking about in today's text. The first two verses set the tone:

*"**If you listen obediently** to the Voice of God, your God, and heartily **obey all his commandments** that I command you today, God, your God, will place you on high, high above all the nations of the world. All these blessings will come down on you and spread out beyond you because you have responded to the Voice of God, your God"* (Deuteronomy 28: 1-2, MSG).

Huge promises, magnificent fireworks, all tidied-up nicely with two looming *"ifs."* Yeah, there's the catcher—one had to *obey*.

The next twelve verses show the seriousness of God's intent to bless His people. Storehouses of blessing, the enemy pummeled, and abundant favor is literally everywhere! I mean Sam's Club can't touch this place! Truly, a land flowing with milk and honey... IF you had the stuff it took to *obey* completely!

Beginning with verse 15 until the end of the chapter, you go into a dark, thundering rain of curses, sickness, and death.

Jesus, the Christ, should have been the most welcomed sight Israel had ever seen!

In one, single act of submission to his Father's will, He ushered us out from under the Law of sin and death (Romans 8:1-5), free to enter into a new covenant, a better covenant! It's not the old Mosaic covenant reworked either. This is a totally different and new covenant! It's a covenant in His blood (Luke 22:20; Hebrews 8:6-13), designed exclusively for our freedom, life, and power in His Kingdom!

No longer was the blessing tied to a place, a land, or keeping all the rules. This new kingdom can exist anywhere, at any time... especially NOW!

It's a kingdom that cannot be shaken (Hebrews 12:28), full of power (1 Corinthians 4:20), consisting of righteousness, peace, and joy in the Holy Spirit (Romans 14:17). How is this possible?

Because this kingdom is inside of us, on us—all around us!

"Once, having been asked by the Pharisees when the kingdom of God would come, Jesus replied, 'The kingdom of God does not come with your careful

*observation, nor will people say, 'Here it is', or 'There it is', because **the kingdom of God is within your midst**'"* (Luke 17:20-21, NIV).

In The Pages

When you hear the word "GOD," what image fills your mind? What are the qualities that you associate with that image? Are they healthy images that inspire and prop up your spirit of freedom? Why or why not?

Sweet Sleep

August 3
Proverbs 3

"When you lie down, you will not be afraid; when you lie down, your sleep will be sweet." Proverbs 3:24, NASB

"You will lie down, with no one to make you afraid, and many will court your favor." Job 11:19, NIV

The broad lesson put forth here by Wisdom is that there are dividends to being kind and generous to mankind. Some are large and obvious; others are hidden pleasures. We may not even realize how much of a blessing they are to us until something disrupts us, and our life-rhythms get out of synch. Sound and undisturbed sleep is one of those beautiful benefits!

One of the great joys of watching newborn babies sleep is that they sleep without every really knowing stress, agitation, or the complexities of relationships. They don't have to worry about a job, a mortgage, disease, war, the stock market, or the constant threat of nuclear annihilation by some nut job or rouge political faction pissed at the "Great Satan". They just fall asleep and stay there until their soggy diapers and growling tummies rouse their tiny eyelids.

A recent article I perused online reported a conservative estimate that Americans spend close to 20 billion dollars in prescription and over-the-counter sleep aids in a single year. A quarter of our population reports chronic issues with insomnia. These numbers don't even take into account our other sleep remedies: new beds, sound machines, alcohol, more sex, warm milk and cookies. Clearly we've got some issues.

In Job 11, Zophar suggests to Job that he get his moral deficiencies cleaned up in order to get some peace back into his life. Job takes exception to the suggestions, not because the principle is askew, but because his friends have ALL assumed he must have sinned for such horrific results to manifest in his life.

Zophar reveals in his own diatribe that there are two faces of Wisdom, one that man sees, and another known only to the Lord:

"If only he would tell you the secrets of wisdom, for true wisdom is not a simple matter. Listen! God is doubtless punishing you far less than you deserve" (Job 11:6, NLT).

That seems to be what King Solomon is passing on here. We can't live in fear and chronic anxiousness. We are to treat everyone with the same grace that has been extended to us, and trust that God sees and knows all about us.

There are no guarantees that we won't experience pain and tragedy on this planet, but we can believe that He sees us and loves us. God does bless us, but we bless ourselves by serving those around us, by loving those who don't feel they are worthy of our love, and by trusting the goodness of God.

It's kind of like going outside to play when you know all of your homework is done. It allows freedom and internal rest. Peterson's translation says,

"You'll take afternoon naps without a worry, you'll enjoy a good night's sleep" (Proverbs 3:24, MSG).

Time for nite-nite!

In The Pages

Another good word to consider here is harmony. Are you in harmony with man and with the Lord? How "at peace" are you internally? Do you sleep well?

Hupŏtassō's Magic

August 4
Proverbs 4

"Hear, my son, and receive my words; and the years of thy life shall be increased, that the resources of thy life may be many." Proverbs 4:10, Brenton LXX English

I'm staring at this verse today with a bit of a nostalgic reverb. I wonder if young people (anyone under the age of 40) really believe this verse?

We can't change what's in the past, but the only reason I would ever want to go back and redo my '20s and '30s (and no, I'm not looking for Marty McFly's DeLorean), would be to dial in deeper to the hidden needs of my sweet wife, and to better pursue the wisdom of elders (both natural and spiritual).

I was a selfish husband and absentee father for too many years. I was so busy thinking I had all the answers I didn't have ears to hear the words and thoughts of those who had much to teach me. It's not that they (elders) weren't available to me. I just wasn't willing to listen. I wasted many an opportunity to submit and learn.

As I was preparing for a recent sermon, I was reminded that submission to elders is vitally important to normal spiritual growth. The Apostle Peter gives some fairly clear instructions about coming under real pastoral guidance and the loving influence of elders (1 Peter 5:1-11).

Those eleven verses are jam-packed with instructions and reasons why it's so important. It is an incredible gift of direction for all of us. Elders have a responsibility to steward the sheep. It's a holy work that God really cares about.

But in light of today's Proverb, there is an equal amount of responsibility for sons and daughters to posture their hearts to be able to receive what is being offered.

In verse five, Peter addresses the *"younger men."* In the Greek it means *"youthful ones, the new ones, or the fresh things."* He instructs them, *"be subject to your elders."* Again, the original language is quite engaging.

The word **hupŏtassō** (pronounced *hoop-ot-as´-so*) means *"to place yourself under another person's authority."* It's the same word Paul uses when instructing married people to submit to each other's desires in covenant.

Oh, what great things become available to us when we are willing to submit to another person!

As an elder (one of the older guys) in the Lord's service for many years, I know how difficult it is for young adults to wrap their head and heart around these truths. It's sheer magic when a kid really gets this.

Submission gets lots of lip service in our tribe, but very few really want to go the distance in that kind of relational dynamic. Why? Reasons vary, but the impulse to gorge on extreme experience and self-initiation seems to be at an all-time high in modern spiritual culture.

Submission means patience, slowing down, time spent listening to an elder's perspective, and really taking what they say into account. It's rare when a young person embraces this kind of wisdom. But when it happens, the payoff is... simply MAGIC!

In The Pages

Do you *do* the whole submission thing? Is it hard for you, or easy? What are your stereotypes of what it means to submit? Do you know people who have been burned by someone or something they submitted to? What was the real problem (the stuff behind the obvious)?

Cords and Shadows

August 5
Proverbs 5

"The evil deeds of a wicked man ensnare him; the cords of his sin hold him fast." Proverbs 5:22, NIV

"He made a pit and dug it out, and has fallen into the ditch which he made. His trouble shall return upon his own head, and his violent dealing shall come down on his own crown." Psalms 7:15-16, NKJV

When I read *"cords of his sin"* in today's Proverb, I see Lemuel Gulliver lying asleep on that sandy beach, awakening slowly to the realization that the citizens of Lilliput have bound him with their ropes and harnesses. Something or someone of such massive potential ends up captive by the lesser because of a shipwreck.

If ever the solid voice of Wisdom had a cause to warn us, this context would warrant such rhetoric. The entire Proverb is about the illegitimate sexual expressions of adultery and covert physical liaisons. Talk about destruction and bondage! *Cords* and *pits* . . . that is what we should see!

The opening words of today's text are so hypothermic:
Cold and chilling to the bone!

Peterson's translation says, *"The shadow of your sin will overtake you."* If you'll take a moment to read 2 Peter 1:4-9, you see that, because of the change that has happened in us, because of our walk with Christ, we are to no longer be controlled by lust.

He talks about self-control and pushing against the current of a blind culture. And if we're not doing that, we must have our own vision problems.

"For he who lacks these qualities is blind or short-sighted, having forgotten his purification from his former sins" (2 Peter 1:9, NASB).

The blind can't see their own shadow. Which means they're out of touch with their own internal dark spots.

It's amazing how often people who are doing things they know they're not supposed to be doing think they are invisible. Fine, go ahead and believe you're invisible. You're not, and the shadows of sin you are casting are building cords and harnesses that will eventually pin you down.

Dig into the ancient scripture, have a discussion with Haman (Book of Esther), and ask him if he thinks it was a good idea to build the gallows upon that which he intended to have Mordecai hung.

Ask King Saul if he thought visiting the witch of Endor was the right move.

Do you think David wished for a mulligan when it came to Bathsheba?

Or Judas, what about Judas? It was all dirty business, in the shadows.

Don't judge them... learn from them.

In The Pages

Good people doing wrong things usually hide. What are you hiding right now? Are you looking, touching, using, or possessing things that are not good for you? Are you numbed to the effects? Are you aware of your bondage? WHY NOT GET FREE . . . TODAY?!?!

"Today declare and speak life and freedom over your spirit! Command every dark spirit to come under the submission of the blood of Christ, and the Holy Spirit! Pray that today will be a day of deliverance and dispelling of lies. Jesus, turn on the lights and open our eyes! All darkness gone in the mighty name of JESUS!"—MDP 2018

Gagging Down Fruitcake

August 6
Proverbs 6

"For on account of a harlot one is reduced to a loaf of bread, and an adulteress hunts for the precious life." Proverbs 6:26, NASB

In December 2000, Marie Rudisill made her television debut on the Jay Leno Show. At the time, she was this little 89-year-old grandma, affectionately known as the Fruitcake Lady.

Leno often did these segments with her called, *Ask The Fruitcake Lady*, where she would answer offbeat and random questions from the audience that generally just irritated her. Once inflamed, Marie's responses would get so heated, she could make a drill sergeant blush!

I distinctly remember one segment where a young female viewer asked, *"When a man has multiple sex partners, he's referred to as a stud. What do you call a woman when she has multiple sex partners?"* There was no hesitation. Marie snapped, *"Why, she's a whore!"*

It was one of those things you knew you shouldn't be laughing about, but it was so painfully blunt, and coming from such an unexpected source, you couldn't help yourself. Sounds like Marie had a real opinion about sexual promiscuity.

Wisdom addresses a very serious issue in today's text, while still having a bit of fun with us. The word for *harlot* is **zânâh** (pronounced *zaw-naw´*). According to the Strong's Concordance, it means *"highly fed, and therefore promiscuous; to commit adultery (usually of the female, and less often of simple fornication, rarely of involuntary ravishment)"*, and figuratively it holds accusation of *"committing idolatry (the Jewish people being regarded as the spouse of Jehovah)."*

Highly fed? In other words, the *harlot* is giving nothing back to the doofus who is paying her. Oh wait . . . he gets his sexual release. But that's done and dusted in a moment of time. Yet it reduces him to a *loaf of bread*, a piece of fruitcake, the prostitute's source of livelihood.

That's it. That's all he gets out of this deal... maybe.

The second part of this verse ratchets up the consequences. Dealing with a *harlot* is one thing, and there are serious consequences, but now we're talking about a woman who has blatantly ignored her sacred marriage vows and is now on the *hunt* for something to kill and eat.

In spiritual context, this is all about the destruction of something innocent i.e. the *"precious life"*.

The **yâqâr** (pronounced *yaw-kawr'*) was *"the valuable, the brightness, the clear, costly, excellent . . . the precious life."* The *adulterer* is looking for a way to get a cheap infusion. Her or his own miserable existence craves anything that looks and feels like life. To fall prey to their need for blood only creates a vacuum that closes in on death.

Seriously? We'd go there when we can have this:

"Like an apple tree among the trees of the forest, so is my beloved among the young men. In his shade I took great delight and sat down, and his fruit was sweet to my taste. He has brought me to his banquet hall, and his banner over me is love. Sustain me with raisin cakes, refresh me with apples, because I am lovesick. Let his left hand be under my head and his right hand embrace me" (Song of Solomon 2:3-6).

Why would we ever look anywhere else other than our covenant mate?

In The Pages

Married people: are you paying attention? Single people: are you paying attention? What do you get out of today's lesson?

A Waste of the Good Life

August 7
Proverbs 7

"She was always out in the streets or in the city squares, waiting around on the corners of the streets. She grabbed him and kissed him. Without shame she said to him, I made my fellowship offering and took some of the meat home. Today I have kept my special promises. So I have come out to meet you; I have been looking for you and have found you. I have covered my bed with colored sheets from Egypt. I have made my bed smell sweet with myrrh, aloes, and cinnamon. Come, let's make love until morning. Let's enjoy each other's love. My husband is not home; he has gone on a long trip. He took a lot of money with him and won't be home for weeks." Proverbs 7:12-20, MSG

All of Proverbs 7 deals with the ways of an adulterer. Wisdom is making a heartfelt plea to the old and young alike to avoid such entanglements... at all cost!

Although the characterization of the adulterer is packaged in feminine descriptions, no way is it limited to just females.

This is a humanity issue.

Here are some attributes to this person's character: he or she flatters with words (v:5), operates covertly from his or her own home (v:6) looks to exploit youthfulness and innocence (v:7) has plotted and planned how to get what he or she wants (v:10) and has rebelled against his or her own sacred vows (v:11). And that is just the beginning.

Read today's text again. Sobering, isn't it?

As a pastor, I've seen some crazy things. I've witnessed this little charade play itself out more than once. Let me tell you, rarely do I find that these "new couples" live happily ever after, in total peace with themselves.

So much damage and destruction is done to the family unit, especially where kids are involved, it requires years to repair... if it can even be repaired at all.

Secondly, what is birthed in lust is hard to maintain in any kind of real consistency. Stolen bread may taste sweet at the time, but the naïve fail to realize the poison in the dough:

"Stolen water is refreshing; food eaten in secret tastes the best! But little do they know that the dead are there. Her guests are in the depths of the grave" (Proverbs 9: 17-18, NLT).

If you forfeit your family for a new life, with a new mate, who was unfaithful to his or her own duties as husband or wife, how can you ever really trust that person?

If you were miserable in your first marriage, who's to say you won't be miserable in your next one? (It's just a question... not a prophetic declaration.)

All you did was swap addresses and roommates. You haven't changed you. Divorce that happens because of mutual-irreconcilable differences is one thing (and true enough, the damage will be bad), but when a marriage is torn apart by infidelity or adultery, the ramifications are so widespread; it makes building trust a real chore.

If you're single or married, this is serious business to heed. Honestly, the adulterer is up to no good.

Stay home, work out your issues with your mate, forgive, ask for forgiveness, love again, be devoted, open up your heart, and get God in the mix. All that other stuff is a waste of life.

In The Pages

How personally acquainted are you with the damage of infidelity? What additional counsel would you give to people who are being unfaithful in their own marital duties? If you're divorced and remarried, what's different now that has made marriage work for you? If you're single, what did you get out of today's devo?

I realize this devo seems very harsh. I also understand it is usually very complicated when and why marital infidelity happens. People do divorce and can be happily remarried and get on with the rest of their lives. All I'm trying to imply is that divorce is costly in a variety of ways. The grace of God is truly amazing, but some decisions we make demand heavy natural consequences. —MDP 2018.

Favor, Favor, Favor!

August 8
Proverbs 8

"Now therefore, listen to me, my children, for blessed are those who keep my ways. Hear instruction and be wise, and do not disdain it. Blessed is the man who listens to me, watching daily at my gates, waiting at the posts of my doors. For whoever finds me finds life, and obtains favor from the Lord; but he who sins against me wrongs his own soul; all those who hate me love death." Proverbs 8:32-36, NKJV

Maybe one of our biggest oversights when it comes to the value of Wisdom in our lives is the element of *favor*. Most of us consider *favor* to be like privilege. You know, like the privileged, spoiled kid whose parents belong to an exclusive country club. They do as they please, eat what they want, sign the tickets with their membership number, and daddy pays the bills.

That's not what Wisdom is talking about here. This kind of *favor* comes to those who are actively trying to *keep Wisdom's ways* (v:32). It's an enticing thought that should motivate us all.

If you take the time to search it out, you'll find that most of the "big guns" in scripture had this thing about them that facilitated *favor*. The long list of names is as impressive as what they accomplished. Noah (Genesis 6:8), Abraham (Genesis 18:3), Joseph (Genesis 39:4), Moses (Exodus 33:12), Gideon (Judges 6:17), Ruth (Ruth 2:2), Hannah (1 Samuel 1:18), Samuel (1 Samuel 2:26), David (Psalms 30:7, Acts 7:46), Esther (Esther 5:2), Mordecai (Esther 10:3), Daniel (Daniel 1:9), Elizabeth (Luke 1:25), Mary (Luke 1:30), and of course, Jesus (Luke 2:52).

This is not the complete list, but you get the general idea. Even though the things these people accomplished were remarkable, we have to remind ourselves that they were *only* human beings, just like us. Jesus is the only exception.

Wisdom invites us to partake in that same *favor*. We can do this by simply asking for it. These people believed in God for the "big stuff," so they sought after Him, prayed for increase, and it seems He was more than willing to give them what they asked for. I don't know about you, but I want some of God's *favor*!

God, give us favor! Favor, favor, favor!

There's no need to over analyze this. Lady Wisdom promises that God's *favor* is a part of the package when we walk towards the pursuit of wisdom. God doesn't seem too interested in cooperating with stupidity or sloppiness.

He loves us unconditionally, but He's looking to increase us with His *favor* if we'll just give attention to the details with consistency and excellence. Come on! Let's get ourselves into position to receive some serious *favor* from heaven!

In The Pages

How often are you asking God for favor? What do you have going on in your life that could benefit from a little supernatural grace? Pray now, come on!

GOD, I WANT YOUR FAVOR ON MY LIFE!

EMPOWER ME WITH YOUR FAVOR!

Everyone on the planet can tap into this great hope! I've travelled the world. I see God's favor everywhere. Thankfulness might be our greatest "ask" for more! —MDP 2018

It's Good For YOU

August 9
Proverbs 9

"If you are wise, you are wise for yourself, and if you scoff, you alone will bear it." Proverbs 9:12, NASB

"Live wisely and wisdom will permeate your life; mock life and life will mock you." Proverbs 9:12, MSG

There are a lot of isolated Proverbs (like this one) that are constructed so simply, we tend to overlook the weight of their truth. Indeed, today's verse has the appearance of an offhanded comment, but it's full of goodness for our souls.

Wisdom doesn't have to be intricately complex in order to be spot-on. Sometimes it sits there, like a veiled diamond on a cloudy day. Then, when the sun comes out - BAM! Its brilliance can't be contained.

We should get what we can out of it, here and now. It's when we fail to take truth to heart that Wisdom confirms what she has been saying all along. Let's drink her truth in and allow it to warm our innards.

"If you are wise, you are wise for yourself". **You benefit first.** Don't shy away from this to focus on all the other things that will benefit from your pursuit of wisdom. Take a moment to realize that you (yes, YOU) benefit from your own choice to live wisely. The fact that you want God's best for yourself, that God breaks it down so you can digest and process, and the fact that it releases blessing and favor on your life, means that you benefit first!

If we were discussing a healthy diet or an exercise program, who would you say benefits the most? Sure, your spouse, family, and friends will definitely get something out of your newfound vitality and quality of life, but ultimately, you benefit first! It's good for you, and when you realize those benefits to yourself, you'll be motivated to make those healthy habits a permanent part of your life!

It's good to know it's good for you! So wisdom is good for you! You rightly love yourself when you pursue the Lord and *live wisely*!

"If you scoff, you alone will bear it." Ever heard the phrase, "misery loves company"? It's true because bearing the weight of our own failures is heavy and taxing to our soul!

As a part of the Body, we're encouraged to *"bear one another's burdens"* (Galatians 6:2, NASB), even though there isn't a whole lot of clarity about what qualifies as a *burden*. But regardless, if you're guilty of *scoffing* or *mocking*, you will know and feel the retribution of your own sin.

Sure, people may come and put their arms around you, pray for you, and attempt to comfort you, but you will still feel the effects of your own failures. No matter how big or small the overall damage caused, we'll feel the effects of our sins first and others will feel it also.

If you want a sobering study sometime, go do a concordance search on *mocking* and *scoffing*. God is not cool with that nasty character trait. Not in the least.

In The Pages

How would you grade yourself on your intentionality to live wisely? Why? What has to happen to improve?

Killer Winds

August 10
Proverbs 10

"As the whirlwind passeth, so is the wicked no more: but the righteous is an everlasting foundation." Proverbs 10:25, KJV

I can't help myself. I have to take a stab at my own paraphrase here:

"Those who live only to satisfy self have about as much security as a single-wide on the Oklahoma prairie during tornado season. Those who love the Lord, have deep basements, stocked full of supplies, unmoved by nature's worst" (Proverbs 10:25, Paschall Redneck Translation).

As a kid, I'd heard stories about the devastation of tornados, but none of that made much of an impact on me until Tuesday, April 10, 1979, Wichita Falls, Texas. When the super cells developing out of the moist Gulf air converged with a low-pressure front out of Colorado, it formed three large tornados, which came together to form one, giant F4 tornado that ripped through the heart of Wichita Falls.

That beast was a mile wide and left a track of total destruction almost 8 miles long. Fifty-four people were killed that day in Texas. Entire subdivisions were gone, leaving rubble piles and empty foundations in place.

According to the Fujita scale, there were areas where the damage resembled F5 destruction. That's likened to slinging all the pieces off a chess table in a single movement.

Boom! In one moment, there was order.
In the next, everything was gone.

King Solomon must have been familiar with what a tornado could do. Although I would imagine it's a rare sighting in the Middle East (it's a guess), surely Wisdom is speaking from experience.

Sticks, stones, and mud probably didn't offer too much resistance against strong winds. The word for *"whirlwind"* is **çûwphâh** (pronounced *soo-faw'*), from the root word **çûwph** (pronounced *soof*), which means, *"to snatch away, terminate, consume, have an end, or perish."* Strong's Concordance also points to the words: *hurricane, storm, tempest, whirlwind, and Red Sea.*

Sounds like a few fishermen had got themselves caught out in the nasty elements from time to time. Too bad they never had the privilege of the old toothless Bedouin who stands in front of a camera crew describing the sounds of the storm as that of a train. Yes, it always sounds like a train.

People who are intent on living in *wickedness*, without moral scruples, clueless about security in God, are going to suffer when hardship comes. There is a chance that all will be lost... and when it's gone, it's gone. Nothing will remain.

The promise for the seeker and lover of God is that even if devastation comes and wipes away all you've built, the *foundations* will still be in place.

A starting place for new growth and expansion will always remain!

"The righteous is an everlasting foundation." Winds blow and storms howl, but our relationship with the Lord is the deeply dug foundation for a natural and eternal existence! Even the worst cannot take us out.

In The Pages

When was the last time you were scared during a storm? What preventive measures did you take? Are you prone to protect yourself, or move to the window to get a better view? What does that say about you?

Bad Hair—Worse Advice

August 11
Proverbs 11

"A gracious woman retains honor, but ruthless men retain riches." Proverbs 11:16, NASB

No matter how you carve this one up, it still boils down to a comparison between *honor* and *riches*. I think we know which one has God's endorsement. Nothing wrong with *riches* in and of itself, but *honor* might be harder to come by.

There's this reality show on TV about a dad and his sons who run a motorcycle design business. The whole show focuses on their relationships with each other and the amazing bikes they build for special causes.

Over the past couple of years, a breach developed between the dad and one of the sons, who is also a legal partner in the business. The strained relationship spilled into the courts.

Though it was evident both father and son were highly wounded, neither side would back down in order to repair the strained relationship. The dad may have been the most wounded, and the most stubborn.

More than once, I wished I could sit down with both of them for a little chat. What they were fighting for (pride), and against (each other), was absolutely juvenile and utterly ridiculous reasons.

There was one episode where the dad's crew was building a special bike for a well-known and highly successful real estate tycoon who happened to have his own popular television program. In a candidly vulnerable moment, the dad opened up to the wealthy developer about his son suing him. Personally, I was hoping for the tycoon to tell him to *"man up."* Something like, *"Dude, go make up with your son and stop all this nonsense. What you're fighting about isn't worth it. The relationship is what is important. Don't be stupid!"*

That is NOT what happened.

Instead, the ego-infested powerbroker spewed, *"Fight your ass off. Don't give him a penny!"* Frik! All character assessments confirmed in a moment.

Chalk another relational nightmare up to the immature lack of *honor* and over-inflated egos. –Sigh-

The pro's advice was as bad as his hairdo.

So Wisdom compares the *gracious woman* (honorable) to the *ruthless man* (power broker). This isn't about male verses female. Both are easily capable of being *gracious* or *ruthless*. Again, gender isn't the issue here. It's the character inside of a person that determines what is really valuable.

Money is spendable in the hands of the *ruthless* or the *gracious*, but *honor* is much more selective about where it manifest.

Honor *actually tracks with* **graciousness.**

A person who is aware of how much he's been blessed with has a different kind of outlook on life. He is much more willing to make space for those who have deficiencies.

Honesty and integrity are always at the forefront of his desire. You can just tell these people aren't hiding anything from you. They just feel "clean" to you somehow.

In Wisdom's eye, the person who walks and lives in *honor* truly conveys what it means to be rich. Money isn't everything. Sometimes having *riches* means nothing at all.

In The Pages

Which does our culture respect more, honor or riches? What leads you to believe that? What kind of people do you respect the most in life? What are their qualities?

This devo was written in 2012. Un-frikk'n-believable! —*MDP 2018*

Swampy

August 12
Proverbs 12

"A man shall not be established by wickedness: but the root of the righteous shall not be moved." Proverbs 12:3, KJV

"You can't find firm footing in a swamp, but life rooted in God stands firm." Proverbs 12:3, MSG

Slithery. That's the general feeling we get when we hear the word *swamp*. Peterson helps us draw a correlation between the ways of wickedness, and the soupy muck found in south Florida and Louisiana. A primeval water land, filled with all kinds of slithery, wet critters and gnarly varmints.

Although the History Channel's *Swamp People* have found a way to make a living in that brackish land, most of us would be in real trouble if we were left to fend for ourselves in those swamps.

Solomon discusses foundation, contrasting the *righteous* to the *wicked*. Plainly, the *wicked* are without solid foundations. The majority of mainline translations (NASB, NIV, RSV, KJV, NKJV) say this man will *not be established.*

The word in the Hebrew is **kûwn** (pronounced *koon*), and it means, *"to stand erect or perpendicular."* If you're slithering around in compromised integrity, it's hard to walk honorably upright in your spirit and countenance.

A man or woman deeply rooted in God, however, finds both nourishment and stability. There's no slithering here. The deeper the foundations, the more allowance for growth and increase of God's blessing. Wonder why we're so slow to see this?

Jesus said to his disciples,

"The one on whom seed was sown on the rocky places, this is the man who hears the word and immediately receives it with joy; yet he has no firm root in himself, but is only temporary, and when affliction or persecution arises because of the word, immediately he falls away" (Matthew 13:20-21, NASB).

There it is. That's the problem. *He has no firm root in himself.* Sure, he may be happy and filled with all kinds of good intentions, but he has no real grasp on the patience and commitment it takes to develop such deep roots.

This pretty much summarizes the difficulty of discipleship. That's the world I live in. I've seen it happen time after time. Young believers want all the privilege of intimate relationship, but they are unwilling to give up their own absolute independence. The old adage, *"the grass is always greener on the other side of the fence"* seems to constantly be in play.

These well intentioned young men and women who, deep in their hearts, truly desire covering, discipleship, and mentorship, can't stop spinning in activity long enough to allow wisdom and truth to take firm root inside them.

Building foundations, which allows for the trust of authority, has to happen for younger generations. Until those roots get established, there's no firm footing anywhere!

In The Pages

Do you have a voice of authority in your life that you can sit under to gain wisdom and direction from? Did you default to "Jesus" or "The Holy Spirit" as your answer? Is your attitude, "I submit to no man?" Honestly, if that's how you feel, this is a major problem for you. You just haven't figured it out yet.

Butt Ears

August 13
Proverbs 13

"A refusal to correct is a refusal to love; love your children by disciplining them." Proverbs 13:24, MSG.

"Thus you are to know in your heart that the Lord your God was disciplining you just as a man disciplines his son." Deuteronomy 8:5, NASB

"It is for discipline that you endure; God deals with you as with sons; for what son is there whom his father does not discipline? But if you are without discipline, of which all have become partakers, then you are illegitimate children and not sons. Furthermore, we had earthly fathers to discipline us, and we respected them; shall we not much rather be subject to the Father of spirits, and live? For they disciplined us for a short time as seemed best to them, but He disciplines us for our good, so that we may share His holiness. All discipline for the moment seems not to be joyful, but sorrowful; yet to those who have been trained by it, afterwards it yields the peaceful fruit of righteousness." Hebrews 12:7-11, NASB

I've read all three of these verses several times today, and I am totally convinced that love is in most discipline. That's not to say that parents always do it right. I sure as hell haven't always done it right with my natural and spiritual kids. But love demands that parents steward His kids with instruction and *discipline*.

**The key is finding out which buttons to push
in order to get the kid's attention.**

The *NET Bible* quotes R. N. Whybray, who references an ancient Egyptian proverb, which basically asserts that boys have ears on their butts, and they won't listen until they get spanked. I grin because that was definitely true in my case, but that was about the only way for my parents to get my attention as a child.

But I doubt that's an absolute truth for everyone. Some kids actually smile when you spank them, but will totally take heed if they're grounded from television for a week, made to do chores, or a privilege is revoked.

Whatever makes an impression is kind of the point here. Then, once they're listening, you bring some sort of correction and instruction that is helpful to their development. That's how it's done in most cultures today.

Agrarian-based family systems had parents and children living in proximity 24 hours a day. All of life was about receiving instruction. Great care was taken by elders to communicate as clearly as possible.

Life spans were shorter back then. You could be called upon to take over at any time, so you had to be paying attention. It was crucial to your family's survival. Preparation for tomorrow was happening every day.

The overall understanding I want us to walk away with today is that *discipline* is just another part of the love package at home and in our relationship with the Lord. God did not birth us and then leave us to figure life out on our own. In short, He yanks our chains from time to time to get our attention, just like your momma or daddy did when addressing your "butt ears."

One more time: discipline is not the same thing as abuse, so let's not confuse the two. Read Hebrews 12:7-11 (above) one more time for good measure!

In The Pages

Based on today's Hebrews scripture, why does God discipline us? If we're not sons and daughters, what are we? Does God understand our discomfort with being disciplined?

Tranquility

August 14
Proverbs 14

"A tranquil heart is life to the body, but passion is rottenness to the bones." Proverbs 14:30, NASB

"The wicked will see it and be vexed, he will gnash his teeth and melt away; the desire of the wicked will perish." Psalms 112:10, NASB

"I heard and my inward parts trembled, at the sound my lips quivered. Decay enters my bones, and in my place I tremble. Because I must wait quietly for the day of distress, for the people to arise who will invade us." Habakkuk 3:16, NASB

"Bless the Lord, O my soul, and forget none of His benefits; who pardons all your iniquities, who heals all your diseases." Psalms 103:2-3, NASB

Health in one's bones is mentioned all throughout the Book of Proverbs (3:8; 12:4; 14:30; 15:30; 16:24; 17:22). It suggests that our mental and emotional health has a direct influence on our physical health.

The medical community seems to be much quicker now to consider a person's emotional health before they start throwing drugs at the problem. Over the years, I have seen many people correct their physical complications through prayer, forgiveness, and deliverance.

Our culture has to be the most self-medicated people on the planet! We'll pop a pill in a heartbeat. We want the quickest, fastest, easiest fix to what ails us.

In my blunt, yet non-professional opinion, if we dealt with our fears, rejection issues, and anxiety, and if we would confront our emotional and spiritual control issues, we could just about eliminate a large portion of physical complications we've simply accepted as "normal" health.

I'm not saying our pain and afflictions aren't legit. I'm saying, if we dealt with some of the junk inside our heart, we might have a better shot at maintaining the rest of our body. Call me a simpleton if you want, but I believe the scripture has my back on this.

What is a *tranquil heart*? Most of us would think in terms of a beautiful place, where there are no distractions, stress, or interruptions. It would be the peace we feel in that sort of environment.

The Hebrew language takes a different approach in how we should view *tranquility*. The word is **marpê'** (pronounced *mar-pay'*), with the root being **râphâ'** (pronounced *raw-faw'*). We easily recognize that as one of the designations of God, Jehovah Rapha, or the healing God!

The *tranquil heart* is a healed heart.

It has found its remedy, and it is wholesome and placid. It is the heart that has been submitted to some deliverance and yielded to the touch of the Master.

Wisdom emphatically states that this brings life to the entire body! These people live in such peace, they invite us to rest when we are with them. They never ask; you just feel their rest wrap around you like a warm blanket! Oh, what spiritual implications to us!

The polar opposite brings rottenness, decay, and even death. The Hebrew meaning of *passion* is *"jealous envy."* It's the stuff, which never allows us to be satisfied with what we have. It totally sucks the life right out of us!

In The Pages

When you get emotionally "wacked out" with stress, does it manifest in your body? How? Migraines? Sick to bed? Have you ever considered the possibility of spiritual roots to disease in our bodies? What are your thoughts on that?

The Big "IF"

August 15
Proverbs 15

"He who listens to a life-giving rebuke will be at home among the wise." Proverbs 15:31, NIV

"The ear that hears the rebukes of life will abide among the wise." Proverbs 15:31, NKJV

"He whose ear listens to the life-giving reproof will dwell among the wise." Proverbs 15:31, NASB

Generally, we don't consider any kind of rebuke to be *"life-giving."* Maybe it's just me, but I don't think most "Jesus people" handle rebuke very well.

Maybe it's our own rejection issues or how the rebuke is delivered, but overall, we suck at receiving reproof. That's sad, because Wisdom says there is *life* in that correction. Even the scoffer or fool who desperately needs the rebuke can benefit. Even if the correction is delivered poorly, we still have the opportunity to allow its truth to permeate us.

Sugar does help the medicine go down, but sometimes medicine is just medicine, and we still have to be able to swallow it. The willingness to receive correction is indeed rare, but Lady Wisdom promises that those who are willing to hear will *"dwell among the wise."* It might be one of the greatest compliments Wisdom can give us, **IF** we're willing to listen and take the *rebuke* to heart.

But... that is a big "IF!"

There is something wonderfully magnificent about the person who can take correction, apply the correction, and not be offended in the process. It says a lot about a person's character, and foremost, his or her walk with God.

If we're unapproachable, standing firm and rigid in our positions, unwilling to allow any kind of rebuke to get to our hearts, something in us needs some serious spiritual attention. Scripture is loaded with the idea that discipline, rebuke, and reproof are a normal part of healthy relationships.

If your five-year-old is blowing bubbles in his milk while the family is bowed in prayer, a simple course correction might be all that is needed, and you can do it while keeping a smile on everyone's face! There doesn't have to be bloodshed in order for people to change their minds and hearts.

Living things poop, and living things clean up those messes before any long-term damage is done. Love, life, community, and relationship demand honest encounters and correction.

If you're unwilling to engage in either role, you're actually preventing yourself and others from walking in freedom. Wisdom lovingly encourages us to do the work! It's the only way to maintain a spot in the *abode of the wise*!

In The Pages

So think about the last time someone attempted to correct you. How did you do? Did you cloud up and rain on the attempt, or did you really dial in and listen? Were you too busy defending yourself? Did you intentionally inflict wounds in return because you felt you were being attacked? If you needed to bring correction to another person, would you want them to act the way you acted when you were last corrected? What needs to change?

Pursued By Loyal Love

August 16
Proverbs 16

"Unfailing love and faithfulness make atonement for sin. By fearing the LORD, people avoid evil." Proverbs 16:6, NLT

"By mercy and truth iniquity is purged: and by the fear of the Lord men depart from evil." Proverbs 16:6, KJV

What a powerful verse! Again, I think the King has gone prophetic here, referencing the inconceivable future transaction where the Godhead would provide for our atonement (to cover and cancel the power and guilt of sin). No longer does the blood of bulls and goats account for our good (Hebrews 10:4). The blood, *HIS* blood, the blood of *THE* Lamb, has covered it all!

What a glorious and triumphant display of His heart for us!

Solomon calls it *"unfailing love"* or **cheçed** (pronounced *kheh'-sed*) meaning, *"loyal love."* God's love for us is without measure! Pardon me while I do a little happy dance!

How would you get the attention of the most powerful man on the planet? Nebuchadnezzar was the biggest, baddest alpha-dog around. Nations quaked at the threat of a confrontation. Babylon was a force to be reckoned with, and the king was certainly running the show!

Shortly after that whole furnace incident with Daniel and his buddies, where they showed the king the power of their God, King "Nebby" makes a declaration, acknowledging God's existence and the undeniable signs he had just seen.

"King Nebuchadnezzar sent this message to the people of every race and nation and language throughout the world: 'Peace and prosperity to you! I want you all to know about the miraculous signs and wonders the Most High God has performed for me. How great are his signs, how powerful his wonders! His kingdom will last forever, his rule through all generations.' " (Daniel 4:1-3, NLT)

That's all good and dandy, but just because you declare the goodness of God, doesn't necessarily mean you worship Him and are willing to surrender your plans and agendas for captaining your own ship.

The King was still running the show according to his own script, and some of what was going on was unrighteous. Something had to change. Like the skilled work of a chiropractor, Nebby was about to get the adjustment of a lifetime.

Can we get one thing straight? Without God's interference, without Him actively and constantly pursuing us, we would all be screwed!

Your relationship with the Father works because *He first loved you* (1 John 4:19). Not the other way around. HE opened your heart and eyes. If He hadn't, you'd still be blind and on no telling what kind of path!

So God gives Nebby a dream that turns his world upside down (Daniel 4:4-18). Freaking out, the king calls Daniel in to make sense of it for him (Daniel 4:19-27). This Daniel kid had some serious huevos!

He told the king, *"Therefore, O king, may my advice be pleasing to you: break away now from your sins by doing righteousness and from your iniquities by showing mercy to the poor, in case there may be a prolonging of your prosperity"* (Daniel 4:27, NASB).

You have to read the rest of the chapter to see it, but King Nebby had a radical encounter that transformed his heart. Truth and divine love wrecked his life for the good. No longer did he see himself as a self-made man, but one who had been through a bit of fire himself.

God had been with him and brought him through. In the words of a man who was touched by mercy, *"Now I, Nebuchadnezzar, praise, exalt and honor the King of heaven, for all His works are true and His ways just, and He is able to humble those who walk in pride" (Daniel 4:37, NASB).*

In The Pages

How did you realize you needed the Lord? Was there mystical interference that got your attention? What were your first impressions of God once he had your heart?

Pinned by Love

August 17
Proverbs 17

"A friend loves at all times, and a brother is born for adversity." Proverbs 17:17, NIV

I did not know Ross A. McGinnis[2], but I have been in communication with his parents. Today, I want us to prayerfully read and take in why this young man is being honored.

Medal of Honor Citation

President George Bush presents the Medal of Honor to the parents of Ross McGinnis.

For conspicuous gallantry and intrepidity at the risk of his life above and beyond the call of duty:

Private First Class Ross A. McGinnis distinguished himself by acts of gallantry and intrepidity above and beyond the call of duty while serving as an M2 .50-caliber Machine Gunner, 1st Platoon, C Company, 1st Battalion, 26th Infantry Regiment, in connection with combat operations against an armed enemy in Adhamiyah, Northeast Baghdad, Iraq, on December 4, 2006. That afternoon his platoon was conducting combat control operations in an effort to reduce and control sectarian violence in the area. While Private McGinnis was manning the M2 .50-caliber Machine Gun, a fragmentation grenade thrown by an insurgent fell through the gunner's hatch into the vehicle. Reacting quickly, he yelled "grenade," allowing all four members of his crew to prepare for the grenade's blast. Then, rather than leaping from the gunner's hatch to safety, Private McGinnis made the courageous decision to protect his crew. In a selfless act of bravery, in which he was mortally wounded, Private McGinnis covered the live grenade, pinning it between his body and the vehicle and absorbing most of the explosion. Private McGinnis' gallant action directly saved four men from certain serious injury or death. Private First Class McGinnis' extraordinary heroism and selflessness at the cost of his own life, above and beyond the call of duty, are in keeping with the highest traditions of the military service and reflect great credit upon himself, his unit, and the United States Army.

Spc. McGinnis was 19 years old.

There are many ways to develop today's wisdom message. But what I want us to take away today is simple: friends, family, brothers, and sisters do what is necessary to protect each other when danger, *adversity*, and storm winds blow. We need to appreciate the real friends we have and dedicate ourselves to being better to them in return.

In The Pages

http://www.arlingtoncemetery.net/ramcginnis.htm

http://www.army.mil/medalofhonor/mcginnis/

The McGinnis family recommends for donations:
http://www.woundedwarriorproject.org

Patti and I visited the gravesite of Ross McGinnis at Arlington National Cemetery in 2012. Such a sacred place truly invokes a deep sense of sadness and gratefulness for the multitude of individuals who are laid to rest there. As I walked through the rows of white marble crosses near Ross' grave, many of the stones had recent pictures of the deceased. So many young and beautiful faces of our soldiers who lost their lives while serving America. From the top to the bottom, we owe the best we have to offer to their memory. We owe our best efforts to be the best lovers of humanity we can possibly be. Love holds more answers than war. —MDP 2018

Garden Friends

August 18
Proverbs 18

"A person who has friends may be harmed by them, but there is a friend who sticks closer than a brother." Proverbs 18:24, NET

This isn't an advertisement to protect yourself from your lame friends. I mean, yesterday we read about a young man who laid down his life, literally, for friends. I doubt any of those people were life-long friends, but guys he cared about enough to do something unique and rare. Military guys do "brotherhood" pretty quick.

Ultimately, Wisdom is reminding us to pay attention to the real *friends* we do have. Friendships develop and are maintained at a variety of levels. There are those I call Barney friends. You're nice to them, they're nice to you (like the people you work with), but you'd never really let them into your personal mix or be willing to venture into theirs.

Then, there are your good friends. People you used to be around on a regular basis, but now distance or busy schedules have reduced your time together to an occasional email or text to say, "I miss you." When you get with them, it's like the old days, but it doesn't happen often.

Then you have great friends, best friends, your "garden friends." These are people who are all up in your grill on a regular basis. You think about vacations together, plan life and face the future with hopes of doing it in proximity with a shared and equal commitment. If it goes exclusive, we're talking marriage. It's a relationship that is going to stick, no matter what.

Did you notice I used the words "garden friends"? This is the term I believe truly conveys today's Proverb.

The first use of the word *friends* is **rêya'** (pronounced *ray'-ah*) meaning, *"an associate."* The second use, the *"friend who sticks closer than a brother,"* is **âhab** (pronounced *aw-hab'*), which means, *"to have affection for."* Now we're talking about people we really love and care about.

These are the people who will go the distance with you, no matter what cards you're dealt. No matter how ugly it gets, nothing runs them off. They are with you, for you, standing beside you, regardless of their own demise.

We need people like this! When Jesus went to the garden in Gethsemane to pray, he took Peter, James, and John (Mark 14:32-34). These were his boys, guys who were all up in his chips. He loved everyone, but something was just different with these three.

They were his "garden friends." They couldn't fix anything that was about to happen, but He took comfort in the fact that they were there with Him (even in their weakness) while He pressed the issue with his Father.

This friend can be your lover, your parents, a sibling, best friend, or indeed the *friend who is closer than a brother*. Whoever it is, he or she is a major blessing in your life! We owe some gratitude for such gifts.

Tell those people, *"I love you,"* today! It's important.

In The Pages

Time gets away from all of us. Does your garden friend(s) know what they mean to you? Who needs the same kind of staying power from you? Do they need your words, or just your presence? Pray and prophesy over your friends today. Speak the life of the Kingdom over their heart.

Ka-ching!

August 19
Proverbs 19

"When you're down on your luck, even your family avoids you—yes, even your best friends wish you'd get lost. If they see you coming, they look the other way—out of sight, out of mind." Proverbs 19:7, MSG

At your earliest convenience, pick up a copy of *Same Kind of Different As Me*, by Ron Hall and Denver Moore. It's about a unique friendship that develops between a person who lives on the street, and a couple with substantial means. Yeah, you need to know that story.

Wisdom is just stating the obvious here. It's not an endorsement, a compliment, or a rebuke. It is what it is. Wisdom confirms elsewhere,

"The poor is hated even by his neighbor, but those who love the rich are many" (Proverbs 14:20).

This isn't rocket science. Rich is easy; poor is hard. And for those of us who desire to bring Kingdom here and now, this is a real here-and-now problem.

What do we do? Do we throw money at it? Ignore it? What? Poverty can be such an injustice!

What DO we do about it?

Once upon a time, while attending a chapel service at the Seminary where I was studying, the guest speaker was this guy who had started a ministry that worked with "street people" in downtown Ft. Worth. I felt convicted by his message and started going down there to see how I could help.

Talk about being a duck-out-of-water. Wow, I was frikk'n clueless! I think I went home the first night without my watch, my coat, a cap, the sweatshirt I had on under the coat, and my tennis shoes.

No, seriously! This group sized me up, figured me out in no time, and started placing their orders. Ka-ching!

That was the only thing I could think to do. None of the leaders of that ministry said a word, so I didn't think I was doing anything wrong.

When I showed up the next week, I was intercepted as I approached the table where they were serving Kool-Aid and frozen pizzas (the pizza was actually frozen - not cooked).

"Hey big guy, can I talk to you a second?" I was sure they had a job or something like that for me to do.

"Dude, you can't be giving away all your stuff down here. It's a black hole of need. These people definitely need food and clothes, but they need friends more. Everybody who knows them has rejected these people. They need some love. They'll pimp you if you're only here because of guilt. They've already read you. Keep your stuff, and give away some love."

Honestly, when I was 29 years old, full of myself, with grand ideas of how my ministry was going to rock the world's face off, I was void of any interest in just giving away "some love," as that guy put it—especially when it came to the poor.

I was too distracted to develop relationships with people less fortunate than myself. I had mountains to climb and dragons to slay. The poor were not on my radar at all.

Yep, it's challenging to love on the poor and think you can make any kind of difference. But maybe that's where you'll find your greatest fulfillment in life.

You've probably prayed enough. It might be time to DO something like give away some love!

In The Pages

People with mercy gifts usually thrive around the poor, but the rest of us need to sensitize a bit. Do you have poor family members? When is the last time you checked in on them? How do you love on a friend who is struggling financially?

Thrones of Justice

August 20
Proverbs 20

"A king who sits on the throne of judgment winnows all evil with his eyes." Proverbs 20:8, NRSV

"To show partiality to the wicked is not good, nor to thrust aside the righteous in judgment." Proverbs 18:5, NASB

I wonder what Solomon was thinking when he wrote these words. It's as if he was telling himself, *"I must be just. I must be fair. I must do what is right. Partiality is not an option. I am bound to this. I am bound to this. As God is my witness, I am bound to this."*

Talk about pressure... Wowzers!

Until today, I haven't given a single thought to Karla Faye Tucker since 1998, when she was executed. Wikipedia will give you the entire scoop, but the short version is that a jury of peers sentenced Karla to death for her involvement in a couple of pickaxe murders in 1983.

She was the first woman to be executed in the United States since 1984, and the first in Texas since 1863. Because of her gender and widely publicized conversion to Christianity, she inspired an unusually large national and international movement advocating the commutation of her sentence to life imprisonment, a movement which also included a few foreign government officials.

Karla's transformation had indeed been drastic and consistent. The last couple of years before she was executed, support for her grew among several national government figures, televangelists, and even the international community.

Still, all pleas for retrial and clemency were denied. Even the Governor of Texas took some heat when he denied her request for a 30-day stay of execution. Many in the evangelical community were hoping the Governor's own spiritual convictions would influence him to grant preference to Karla's request, because of her gender and apparent spiritual transformation.

The Governor issued this statement from the State Capitol minutes before her death:

"The role of the state is to enforce our laws and to make sure all individuals are treated fairly under those laws. The courts, including the United States Supreme Court, have reviewed the legal issues in this case, and therefore, I will not grant a 30-day delay. May God bless Karla Faye Tucker, and may God bless her victims and their families."

On February 3, 1998, at 6:45pm, Karla Faye Tucker was pronounced dead from the lethal injection carried out by the state.

There is a good chance you're reading this with a fairly strong opinion about how all that went down. My point today is not to render a right or wrong verdict. My hope is to encourage us to see the "pressure" that is placed squarely upon the shoulders of the lawyers, judges, and law enforcement officials who have to *winnow* through our gigantically cumbersome judicial system with equity and non-partiality.

They take a lot of flak—a lot of ridicule and disrespect. But the weight they carry, and the responsibility they bear is a necessary burden that benefits us all in the long run!

May God grant them the Wisdom to see what needs to be seen, and the courage to uphold all pillars of justice!

In The Pages

Do you ever pray for anyone in the judicial system? Do you pray for the Supreme Court Justices or the Attorney General? Are you up to speed on what kind of cases the higher courts are reviewing in this country? Are you aware of what God is doing inside of the prison systems across America? Check it out. It's pretty cool.

Wandering into Sheol

August 21
Proverbs 21

"A man who wanders from the way of understanding will rest in the assembly of the dead." Proverbs 21:16, NASB

"This is the way of those who are foolish, and of those after them who approve their words. Selah. As sheep they are appointed for Sheol; Death shall be their shepherd; and the upright shall rule over them in the morning, and their form shall be for Sheol to consume so that they have no habitation." Psalms 49:13-14, NASB

All this talk of *death* and *Sheol* is such a drag, but we'd all be much better off if we could get our hearts and minds wrapped around today's wisdom.

The problem is our periodic appetites to *wander*.

Let's look at the Hebrew. **Tâʿâh** (pronounced *taw-aw´*) means, *"to vacillate, reel or stray."* It can also mean, *"to go astray, to deceive, to dissemble; also to cause to err, pant, seduce, stagger, or be out of the way."* So we're not talking about the globetrotting adventurer here.

This is a person who knows better but has made a choice to stray from some solid foundation, anchor, or source of stability. The results aren't good. In fact, someone or something is going to have firsthand knowledge of the gates of hell on earth.

I realize that most of you who read this devotional are NOT the stereotypical Evangelical Christians. I suspect you're a little edgy, wired differently, and particularly dialed in to hearing the voice of God.

I've been writing this stuff for a couple years now (2010-2012), and often I've thought this material really isn't Granny's devotional. To be honest, most of the devos I've written have been inspired by real scenarios that I've tried to recount for you as honestly as possible. I've tried not to filter too much. I figure that part is obvious.

I received this text about 30 minutes ago from a spiritual daughter:

Her: *You alive?*

Me: Yup ;) On vaca wid fam. U good?

Her: *Yeah, I wanted to see if possibly my friends could talk to you and Patti... I think they found someone to talk to today, but maybe when you're off your vacation. Her husband just told her he has been having an affair with his secretary...no sex, so he says, but inappropriate talking and touching. They are the couple I lead high school kids with at church.*

Me: Yuck!

Her: *Yeah... he is the last person I would have ever thought... I just feel so bad for her.*

Me: See Proverbs 21:16. Call me later. xo

See? Real stuff. This is what happens when a person *"wanders from the way of understanding"*.

You don't have to make this stuff up.

In The Pages

Can you just soak in this for a minute and pray for the troubled marriages you know about? There is pain coming in this. Can you feel it?

Doin' The King

August 22
Proverbs 22

"He who loves a pure heart and whose speech is gracious will have the king for his friend." Proverbs 22:11, NIV

"Whoever secretly slanders his neighbor, him I will destroy; no one who has a haughty look and an arrogant heart will I endure. My eyes shall be upon the faithful of the land, that they may dwell with me; he who walks in a blameless way is the one who will minister to me." Psalms 101:5-6, NASB

If there was ever evidence direct from the horse's mouth, it's this little passage from David's Psalm! People of power are running assessments of character. Solomon has also opened his heart. He has revealed something very intimate here. With all the pressures of his role as Israel's leader, and with being surrounded by strong men with strong agendas, the man needed some serious time with people of depth and grace. David had the same need and desires.

David says that few are those *"who will minister to me"*. Of course he needed strong and assured counsel around, but what about when he got really tired? What about that empty fatigue that sets in and has you questioning everything about your life? You can't let just anyone see that, especially when you're in a position of power and people are looking to you. You need something else—*someone* else.

You need strength, but it needs to be a strength that actually loves and cares about you, not just your influence or the mission. Yeah, it's a rare find, but every now and then, you'll find that Jonathan who will remind you of the truth about yourself, even though you don't believe it in that moment.

They ooze grace-filled words. They're not patronizing or schmoozing you. It's coming from the heart. It's pure refreshment to your fatigued and thirsty soul.

Early on in my ministerial profession, I learned that just because a person quotes you scripture or a Proverb doesn't necessarily mean it's coming from a good heart, or a right spirit. One particular person I'm thinking of made it their personal mantra to say (quite often), *"A gentle answer turns away wrath" (Proverbs 15:1)*. Evidently, they decided that whispering was the best way to communicate this.

This person's outward appearance was always reserved and under control. At first, I thought that this was one of the most pure things I had ever seen. But, with time, I began to realize that it wasn't coming out of grace at all. It was a strategy.

It was a passive-aggressive control mechanism. It wasn't graceful. It was for their own benefit—to make them look good.

> **Once you realize you've been sucked into a game,
> you don't want to play anymore!**

You don't want to open up anymore. You don't want anything else from that person. Being that person's pastor required me to have to be frank and brutally honest about the juice coming off their religious method.

Being a "David" or "Solomon" meant you gave limited access, if any at all. The opportunity to touch and love the King was a rare privilege. Could it be that there is an even bigger message for us all to glean?

In The Pages

Do you run games with people? Are you just being nice, or do you have ulterior motives? Are you seeking to truly minister to leadership, or just looking for another opportunity to be seen, heard, or noticed? Are you a real friend?

Buying Different

August 23
Proverbs 23

"Buy the truth, and do not sell it, also wisdom and instruction and understanding." Proverbs 23:23, NKJV

"You must not follow the crowd in doing wrong. When you are called to testify in a dispute, do not be swayed by the crowd to twist justice." Exodus 23:2, NLT

Before you dive into this today, go back and read Exodus 23:1-8. It will give you some perspective.

Today's text creates a bit of a paradox for us. The ancient voices of wisdom make a turn in their "sayings" a few verses earlier.

Up until Proverbs 23:13, all the dialogue has been educational and inspirational. Then today's Proverb leads us down a path that is a bit more aggressive!

When the ancients tell us to *"buy the truth,"* they mean to do whatever is necessary to acquire wisdom. Spare no expense, make every effort to have it, use it, and put it to work for you.

Then they say, *"and do not sell it,"* which means we are to place it at the top of our food chain and let it be a life priority. Do not compromise its integrity, do not cheapen it, nor allow the wisdom we have to be distorted and polluted by streams of contrasting values.

I immediately think of when Jesus said, *"The kingdom of heaven is like a treasure hidden in the field, which a man found and hid again; and from joy over it he goes and sells all that he has and buys that field"* (Matthew 13:44, NASB).

To this man, that treasure was priceless, so he went and sold everything in order to acquire his prize!

The voice of the ancients came with the same kind of passion about our acquiring wisdom. It's probably more valuable to us that we realize.

On my first trip across the pond to the UK, a missionary friend told me a funny story one day as we were walking though a picturesque village. As we peered into the window of a small mom-and-pop appliance store, he told me that he had been in that store a few days earlier trying to by an oscillating fan.

The only fan they actually had in the whole store was the fan on the display counter. When my buddy realized none were in stock, he offered to buy the fan on display. The owner wouldn't sell it.

He said, *"If I sell it to you, then I won't have a fan on my shelf anymore."* My friend stood scratching his head with a "WTH" look on his face and then giggled his way out of the store. Guess there is more than one way to do business?

Earlier I mentioned a paradox. We've already touched on it some, but if you're going to "go the distance" with wisdom, you're going to have to face whether or not you're going to allow it to shape your value system. The *crowd* always has its own current, another thought, or a different way.

Pop culture, trend setters, artists, poets, politicians, preachers, media types, Hollywood, Wall Street, Nashville, whoever the hell it is—all of them have a frikk'n opinion!

The latest ain't always the greatest!

Maturity makes room for truth, and it is rarely enamored with the shallowness of the most popular streams of culture's opinion.

In The Pages

How serious have you been in your personal search for and acquisition of wisdom? How often do you pray for insight and application of wisdom? How do you best value wisdom in your own life? In others' lives?

Tapped In

August 24
Proverbs 24

"I passed by the field of one who was lazy, by the vineyard of a stupid person; and see, it was all overgrown with thorns; the ground was covered with nettles, and its stone wall was broken down. Then I saw and considered it; I looked and received instruction. A little sleep, a little slumber, a little folding of the hands to rest, and poverty will come upon you like a robber, and want, like an armed warrior." Proverbs 24:30-34, NRSV

If the *Sayings of the Ancients* (Proverbs 22:17- Proverbs 24:34) are likened to a liturgical worship service, today's verses are a fitting postlude. In a very intimate exposure of thought and reason, the writer allows us a peek into a very simple accounting of something he noticed. He then reflected on it, and ultimately drew some conclusions about what he had witnessed.

I like the progression in verse 32 where he says he *saw*, he *considered*, he *looked*, and he *received*. What is happening here is much more spiritually charged than we might imagine.

It's more than just a guy walking by a dilapidated vineyard, making flippant judgments about the lazy, good-for-nothing owner, only to pass by unbothered or unmoved by what he saw. When I say, "spiritually charged," I mean this guy tapped into a prophetic vein here.

Something in the scene touched him. We have no idea what it was exactly, but seeing the overgrowth of natural encroachment, and the neglect of something that was once useful and productive, stirred this writer, and unlocked a download in the Spirit that we now affectionately call Wisdom. I believe the conclusions he drew concerning what he witnessed are good and right.

Peterson's translation says, *"You can look forward to a dirt-poor life, with poverty as your permanent houseguest"* (Proverbs 24:34, MSG). True enough. But again, this ancient voice had drilled into a deep well of processed revelation. We should suppose that this was normal for him and that is why it makes him unique.

Not everyone is willing to tap into the Spirit like this.

And considering that the overall lesson today is about laziness, it could be that we aren't willing to tap into the revelatory gifts because we are not willing to take the time for instruction to manifest. So many religious Christians stomp through life like the Texas Aggie Marching Band. Everything is controlled, coordinated, and calculatedly precise.

We know all the rules, we know where the boundary lines are located, and we have numbered steps and agendas to let us know how well we are doing. Life in the Spirit, life that desires the riches of God's presence, suggests that we stop stomping.

There are seasons of waiting for His instructions, listening with our hearts, trusting and believing by faith, and living in a hungry openness to receive what He wants us to have. And then there are seasons of quiet that test our resolve to trust what we can't hear or see.

With all of that said, I believe the encounter we read about today is the marvelous expression of a man or woman who desires to tap into prophetic goodness of life's most simple things. How much do we not see simply because we are not tapped in to the Spirit?

In The Pages

What do you think it means to tap into the Spirit? How often do you engage in the process? Are there benefits to you personally? What are they?

Heap It Up

August 25
Proverbs 25

"If your enemy is hungry, give him food to eat; if he is thirsty, give him water to drink. In doing this, you will heap burning coals on his head, and the LORD will reward you." Proverbs 25:21-22, NIV

Whenever I hear this passage burped out of context, it usually has a nasty little aftertaste to it. We think this verse means to *"kill 'em with kindness."*

In other words, we should be so kind and caring, our words so soothing, that our enemies soon realize their errors, fall to their knees, vomit their confessions, and beg us for forgiveness. Then they go with us to the next Sunday School social. Nice.

Frankly, our motivation behind the whole *"kill'em with kindness"* strategy is jacked up, and not what this verse is conveying at all.

Somewhere, back in the day, when I would sit in my nice little walnut veneer-lined office in some little church not on anyone's map, I remember studying this whole *"coals on his head"* thing. It wasn't the punishment we think it is. It was actually a real blessing in those days to have someone give you coals and embers in a bucket that you actually carried on your head.

You could take it home and it was a fire starter of sorts. It was about a real legitimate blessing, not some sort of nasty rebuke that was shrouded in a fake smile or a false joviality.

Does God reward you and I for a hateful-snarky spirit underneath a fabricated smile?

You might win your adversary, and you might diffuse a strained situation, but there is no guarantee in that. You have to be willing to trust that God sees what is real in your heart, and He rewards accordingly.

Sure, you might end up wearing that lasagna you gave to your enemy in a gesture of goodwill, but you will at least have the assurance that your heart was sincere, and you did what was right. God notices that.

We need to be more proactive about these kinds of things. Of course, it requires us to massage this stuff in prayer before we move forward. We get poison stuck in our spirit about people.

Once we give up our grievances and we honestly forgive and release those who have hurt us, we are free to fulfill what Wisdom asks from us. *"And the LORD will reward you."*

Just keep saying it over and over. *"And the LORD will reward you."*

In The Pages

What stops you from taking those first steps in offering peace and reconciliation with a strained relationship? Are you willing to breach the gap of communication and offer a connection, or at the very least willing to pray about it? What are some possible options to show you are interested in blessing from your side?

A Real Tool

August 26
Proverbs 26

"Do you see persons wise in their own eyes? There is more hope for fools than for them." Proverbs 26:12, NRSV

"For the word of the cross is foolishness to those who are perishing, but to us who are being saved it is the power of God. For it is written, **'I WILL DESTROY THE WISDOM OF THE WISE, AND THE CLEVERNESS OF THE CLEVER I WILL SET ASIDE.'** *Where is the wise man? Where is the scribe? Where is the debater of this age? Has not God made foolish the wisdom of the world? For since in the wisdom of God the world through its wisdom did not come to know God, God was well-pleased through the foolishness of the message preached to save those who believe. For indeed Jews ask for signs and Greeks search for wisdom; but we preach Christ crucified, to Jews a stumbling block and to Gentiles foolishness, but to those who are the called, both Jews and Greeks, Christ the power of God and the wisdom of God. Because the foolishness of God is wiser than men, and the weakness of God is stronger than men. For consider your calling, brethren, that there were not many wise according to the flesh, not many mighty, not many noble; but God has chosen the foolish things of the world to shame the wise, and God has chosen the weak things of the world to shame the things which are strong, and the base things of the world and the despised God has chosen, the things that are not, so that He may nullify the things that are, so that no man may boast before God. But by His doing you are in Christ Jesus, who became to us wisdom from God, and righteousness and sanctification, and redemption, so that, just as it is written,* **"LET HIM WHO BOASTS, BOAST IN THE LORD."** *1 Corinthians 1:18-31, NASB*

I hope you realize that today's text may be some of the most liberating words ever written by man! It seems God is not deciding who and what He uses based on external credentials and intellectual accolades.

In fact, if those things become the basis for why you think you're qualified, they actually disqualify you. No, it's not an invitation to be a dumbass.

Prudence is always welcomed inside Kingdom agendas, and that includes educational due diligence and higher learning.

But if you're pompous, arrogant, and prideful about your intellect, you'll find yourself confined, no matter how many diplomas you put on the wall.

God is looking for a tender heart, a soft spirit, an open mind, and someone who can be taught by anyone or anything. If you're so damn smart, reclusive, or socially inept that you can't do people, it will be hard for you to be taught by life's rich experiences.

Believe it or not, *books* don't love, *doctrine* doesn't get filled with the Holy Spirit, and *polity* ain't helping anyone work out his or her faith. If those things are the scope of your passion and interest, public ministry might not be the best place for you to be operating.

The world is waiting on some tender vulnerability, not just another tired formula!

People who are aflame in the love of God know that God digs on brokenness and desperate dependence! These are the tools that God welds in bringing the Kingdom. Can you live with this kind of defacing foolishness?

In The Pages

Please take a moment and go back and read that passage in 1 Corinthians one more time. What one sentence rocks you the most? Why? What, practically, can be done to apply its truth in your life?

Mirror Mirror

August 27
Proverbs 27

"As in water face reflects face, so a man's heart reveals the man." Proverbs 27:19, NKJV

"This is the message you have heard from the beginning: We should love one another. We must not be like Cain, who belonged to the evil one and killed

his brother. And why did he kill him? Because Cain had been doing what was evil, and his brother had been doing what was righteous. So don't be surprised, dear brothers and sisters, if the world hates you. If we love our Christian brothers and sisters, it proves that we have passed from death to life. But a person who has no love is still dead. Anyone who hates another brother or sister is really a murderer at heart. And you know that murderers don't have eternal life within them. We know what real love is because Jesus gave up his life for us. So we also ought to give up our lives for our brothers and sisters. If someone has enough money to live well and sees a brother or sister in need but shows no compassion—how can God's love be in that person? Dear children, **let's not merely say that we love each other; let us show the truth by our actions**. Our actions will show that we belong to the truth, so we will be confident when we stand before God. Even if we feel guilty, God is greater than our feelings, and he knows everything. Dear friends, if we don't feel guilty, we can come to God with bold confidence. And we will receive from him whatever we ask because we obey him and do the things that please him. And this is his commandment: We must believe in the name of his Son, Jesus Christ, and **love one another**, just as he commanded us. Those who obey God's commandments remain in fellowship with him, and he with them. And we know he lives in us because the Spirit he gave us lives in us." 1 John 3:11-24, NLT*

I'm more than content to let the Word speak for itself today! Take a few moments, read these passages several times, and let the verses percolate in your spirit.

It doesn't require a new revelation for us to see the importance of what Wisdom is communicating here. It's the stuff inside our hearts that is the real juice of our lives.

We're easily distracted, caught up in the shallow vanities of pop culture and technological cravings of the "next new thing." But none of those things have anything to do with who and what we really are.

Some of us have never stopped playing "dress up." We do everything we can to protect and project how we want to be perceived. We don't have to get caught up in all that personal marketing and social strategizing. Live honestly from the heart.

Don't JUST talk about your so-called compassion.

BE COMPASSIONATE!

Fine, blog about love... but you need to give away some love in the process. Tweet about the importance of forgiveness, but don't forget to actually be forgiving to the people in this world who have wounded you.

The world, and the people who inhabit it, need access to the real you, whether they realize it or not. We get the real you when it comes from your heart!

Speaking your heart might not be enough. So, live it.

In The Pages

What prevents you from living out what is actually in your heart? What is shutting you down? Do you have anyone that you allow to see the real you? Do they think your life reflects your heart?

The O.C.S.

August 28
Proverbs 28

"An arrogant man stirs up strife, but he who trusts in the Lord will prosper." Proverbs 28:25, NASB

"Greed causes fighting; trusting the Lord leads to prosperity." Proverbs 28:25, NLT

These two translations seem to be saying different things, but they're not. The Hebrew word for *"arrogant"* means *"broad or roomy in any direction."* It can also mean *"proud, wide, or large."*

Generally, this word was used to describe greedy people—people so consumed with their own personal agendas; they pay little (if any) attention to your thoughts, desires, or plans. These are people who are on a mission to get what they want.

They don't care who they have to step on to acquire their goals. They measure success by their own standards.

It's a win-at-all-costs attitude. We kind of expect that sort of behavior in

Western business models, but when it surfaces in our churches or ministries, it's quite sickening.

Wisdom says that the *"arrogant man"*, the greedy person, is a person who doesn't mind "stirring the pot." I like to call these people "Official Crap Stirrers" or the O.C.S. We are warned of members of the O.C.S. all throughout Proverbs. Check out some of the companions of greedy arrogance:

"Who with perversity in his heart continually devises evil, who spreads strife" (Proverbs 6:1, NASB). Lovely. That particular word for *"perversity"* means *"fraudulent and deceitful."*

"Hatred stirs up strife, but love covers all transgressions" (Proverbs 10:12, NASB). Nice.

"A hot-tempered man stirs up strife, but the slow to anger calms a dispute" (Proverbs 15:18, NASB). You depressed yet?

"A perverse man spreads strife, and a slanderer separates intimate friends" (Proverbs 16:28, NASB). Jesus help us!

You get the point?

This person ain't right.

Can't be trusted. He tells you one thing to your face and says something else behind your back. He'll write you checks you can't cash and make promises he can't keep. He's quite frustrating to deal with.

"An angry man stirs up strife, and a hot-tempered man abounds in transgression" (Proverbs 29:22, NASB).

It might be best to just stay out of this person's way until you can find out what he's angry about. If you know, maybe you can offer some assistance. If not, well, better pack a lunch. There's always something bigger going on behind the scenes.

So, there you have it—a fairly accurate, yet less than admirable, picture of the O.C.S. Club. Trust me, you do not want a membership here.

Steer clear at all costs.

You need to do your homework before you build anything with these people. Your religious biases can blind you. Again, it's a problem with religious people because they can play a pious role, and you won't find out the truth until it's too late.

Pray for some discernment!

Big ministries, especially the ones that are business model focused and not people centered, don't necessarily have God's plan for you as a priority. We've got to pull our heads out of the sand when it comes to these people.

In The Pages

How do you help a greedy person? What about the arrogant person? How are your patience levels with these people? People who say they "trust the Lord" can also be arrogant. How well do you know the people you serve alongside in ministry? Are you reading the press clippings they wrote, or do you really know them?

Gettin' Low

August 29
Proverbs 29

"A man's pride will bring him low, but he who is lowly in spirit will obtain honor." Proverbs 29:23, RSV

"The Lord is near to the brokenhearted and saves those who are crushed in spirit." Psalms 34:18, NASB

I've tried not to overlook any passage in Proverbs that has the word *"pride"* in it. Nothing good comes from pride. It leads to all kinds of downfalls—demotions, downward spirals, crash-and-burns.

The only question is how fast, and to what extent, will the destruction occur?

It will happen, sooner or later. It's just a matter of time.

Scripture is full of stories of prideful men. The ones who obtained power, wealth, and status, didn't seem to realize how they got all that power in the first place, or else they forgot. Whenever God intervened in order to get their attention, it usually meant a power encounter of some sorts. Somebody was going to get an ass whipping.

This stuff doesn't just happen in worldly realms. Pride happens inside of God's camp too! Devout Christians, with real Kingdom agendas, can be the most arrogantly prideful people in the whole world.

Do you think there would be more of us (Christians) if our history had been written in humility, instead of pious pride?

Uncomfortably, I think we already know the answer to that question. We build a fancy building, decorate it to our liking, fill it with people, and automatically assume God is in the house. What goofy nonsense is this? We really need to flush that kind of thinking.

This particular word for *"pride"* is **ga'ăvâh** (pronounced *gah-av-aw'*) meaning, *"arrogance or majesty,"* but implies *"ornament, excellence, haughtiness, highness, prideful swelling."*

This isn't just a "punk" we're dealing with here. This is a person who has obtained real status and is living in the *"fullness"* of self-appreciation and narcissistic confidence.

"The king reflected and said, 'Is this not Babylon the great, which I myself have built as a royal residence by the might of my power and for the glory of my majesty?'" (Daniel 4:30, NASB)

That is how a person like this thinks and operates.

The prophet weighs in, *"Behold, as for the proud one, his soul is not right within him" (Habakkuk 2:4, NASB)*. Yup! Pride will jack you up, severely! And when God starts messing with you to sort all that out to make some heart adjustments, you're not going to like it. Trust me! I'm speaking from personal experience.

The Psalm posted today says, *"He is near,"* or draws near (relationally, and in all seasons) to those of us who get down in our spirit. But giving-in to a prideful attitude is only an invitation for some kind of adjustment.

"Pride goes before destruction, and a haughty spirit before a fall"
(Proverbs 16:18, NKJV).

It's not "IF" we fall... it's "WHEN" will we fall?

Which will we choose... honor or humiliation? Surely that's an easy choice for us to make. Right?

In The Pages

If you were to point out an area in your life where you're vulnerable to pride, what would it be? Do you feel justified? Do you feel "off balance" and without peace because of it? Come on, let's give it up and get right!

Zit Puss

August 30
Proverbs 30

"There is a generation that curses its father, and does not bless its mother. There is a generation that is pure in its own eyes, yet is not washed from its filthiness. There is a generation—oh, how lofty are their eyes! And their eyelids are lifted up. There is a generation whose teeth are like swords, and whose fangs are like knives, to devour the poor from off the earth, and the needy from among men." Proverbs 30:11-14, NKJV

Dishonor... hypocrisy... arrogance... and oppression. This is a *generation* exhibiting fatal flaws contrary to Kingdom agenda. If you're guilty in any one of these four areas, you're more than likely guilty of them all.

I won't work it all out for you, but if you spend some time on this, you'll discover this stuff is all linked together. Defilement in one area makes you automatically guilty of the others.

If you adamantly defend that you only speak highly of your parents and treat them with honor, but you're spiritually arrogant, a hypocrite, or controlling and oppressive to others, you've dishonored your parent. Your behavior can be a reflection on them.

It's not always about how you treat them directly. Dishonor can happen indirectly just because you're wearing their name.

We all realize (I hope) that we're no longer under the old Law, but Matthew

15:4-6 reminds us that Jesus referenced Exodus 20:12 implicitly by instructing us that we must honor our parents. Regardless of your age, or their ability to "parent," you had an obligation, a single duty to them:

HONOR.

It's not just about how you treat them in public either. That can be misleading and not quite the whole story. God is looking at the heart. That's the part that can't be fabricated. It always comes back to that... doesn't it?

So let's assume your parents were scumbags—lower than zit puss. They abused, ignored, criticized, controlled, or abandoned you. You feeling loved wasn't even remotely on their radar. How do you honor them, despite the piss-poor job they did raising you?

It's a good question.

Honor doesn't mean that you craft a bed of roses from weeds.

The key here is about you staying out of defilement. To stay out of defilement means you are going to have to forgive the sins of their humanity. If you truly forgive their failures, it means that you do not hold those failures against them now. It means you're open to loving others and willing to be loved back in all the ways you need.

If you let your wounds lead you through life, you'll succumb to defilement. So you've got to forgive and get some healing. Only then can you honestly face the crap you grew up in and not manifest the rejection that so wants to take over your life.

Honoring damaged parents may mean that you don't expose their weaknesses to everyone you meet. Real forgiveness leaves the past out of your future.

You've done the work, and the mention of your parents no longer sends you into a rage of anger and contempt. Settle the big and small issues with your parents so the rest of the stuff in today's verses can get dealt with too.

In The Pages

Once the lights are low and the wine glasses are half-full, how well do you speak of your parents with friends and acquaintances? What would be your parents' assessment of how well you honor them? How can you do a better job of honoring them?

Baddest Dude

August 31
Proverbs 31

"Open your mouth for the mute, for the rights of all the unfortunate. Open your mouth, judge righteously, and defend the rights of the afflicted and needy." Proverbs 31:8-9, NASB

"And Job again took up his discourse and said, 'Oh that I were as in months gone by, as in the days when God watched over me; when His lamp shone over my head, and by His light I walked through darkness; as I was in the prime of my days, when the friendship of God was over my tent; when the Almighty was yet with me, and my children were around me; when my steps were bathed in butter, and the rock poured out for me streams of oil! When I went out to the gate of the city, when I took my seat in the square, the young men saw me and hid themselves, and the old men arose and stood. 'The princes stopped talking and put their hands on their mouths; the voice of the nobles was hushed, and their tongue stuck to their palate. 'For when the ear heard, it called me blessed, and when the eye saw, it gave witness of me.'" Job 29:1-11, NASB

There is deep richness to today's Proverb. If Lemuel was indeed Solomon, we would then assume that the weight of King David's voice over his princely son had been massive! You just know David walked and talked with the swag and pomp of governmental authority.

Solomon's development was, no doubt, shaped by the powerful words and strong heart of his father. But here, we feel a different kind of weight—the weight of a mother stewarding the stuff God really cares about. I see a mom telling her son to be the *voice of the mute*, the *unfortunate*, the *afflicted* and *needy*. I detect the slightest Messianic aroma in it!

Nothing endears a culture to its leader like a right mind and a benevolent heart towards the less fortunate. Not allowing gross injustice to operate on his watch brings security and stability to mankind as a whole. It's a big frikk'n deal! Mom knew what she was talking about.

At one time, Job was the cock of the walk, the baddest dude of the neighborhood! Read Job 29:1-11 again, and ask yourself the question, "Why?"

Why was he so respected, so admired, and so loved by those around him?

"Because I delivered the poor who cried for help, and the orphan who had no helper. The blessing of the one ready to perish came upon me, and I made the widow's heart sing for joy. I put on righteousness, and it clothed me; my justice was like a robe and a turban. I was eyes to the blind and feet to the lame. I was a father to the needy, and I investigated the case which I did not know. I broke the jaws of the wicked and snatched the prey from his teeth" (Job 29:12-17, NASB).

It wasn't his wealth, celebrity, good looks, or charm that made him so loved. Job was valued as a man because he stood for those who could not, or would not, stand for themselves. He was a real advocate for the broken. Sounds like Kingdom to me!

In The Pages

How do you counteract injustice? How do you voice your concern, conviction, or opposition? What does it cost you to stand in your conviction? Do you offer any help to the broken? The poor? The estranged? The innocent?

You Are Going To Die

September 1
Proverbs 1

"Because they hated knowledge and did not choose the fear of the Lord. They would not accept my counsel, they spurned all my reproof. So they shall eat of the fruit of their own way and be satiated with their own devices. For the waywardness of the naive will kill them, and the complacency of fools will destroy them. But he who listens to me shall live securely and will be at ease from the dread of evil." Proverbs 1:29-33, NASB

"But My people did not listen to My voice, and Israel did not obey Me. So I gave them over to the stubbornness of their heart, to walk in their own devices. Oh that My people would listen to Me, that Israel would walk in My ways! I would quickly subdue their enemies and turn My hand against their adversaries. Those who hate the Lord would pretend obedience to Him, and their time of punishment would be forever. But I would feed you with the finest of the wheat, and with honey from the rock I would satisfy you." Psalms 81:11-16, NASB

Have you ever thought about how you want to die? Not the actual dying part, but the condition of your mind and heart when that happens and the influence you had?

What will you be full of at the end of your life?

Have you ever considered that?

"One dies in his full strength, being wholly at ease and satisfied; His sides are filled out with fat, and the marrow of his bones is moist, while another dies with a bitter soul, never even tasting anything good. Together they lie down in the dust, and worms cover them" (Job 21:23-26, NASB).

Yes, the context is different. But this is what I'm referring to when I ask "what will you be full of?" Forget the worms part. That's not what I'm talking about!

Will you be content, full of *"ease,"* and satisfied, or will you be filled with regret, anger, bitterness, and want? How you end is pretty dependent on how you live before that whole process begins, and most particularly, how you live right now. It's good to make some reasonable determinations on the front end.

The personified voice of wisdom makes a bold statement in today's text! I'll paraphrase:

If you'll allow me to speak into your life, we'll manage your today together! You can chill out and stop stressing every little thing that doesn't go your way. You can sleep at night, not worry in the day and walk in absolute confidence that God has your back no matter what! Come on! Doesn't that sound good?

To *"live securely"* means to exist in a place of refuge, safety, and security with feelings of trust. It's not imaginary or fake, but realistic and confident that you're on a journey and in process with the Lord! Yeah, stuff happens, and it's not always rainbows and cupcakes out there. But overall, life is frikk'n awesome!

The promise is "satisfaction" . . . all the way to the very end.

In The Pages

At your wake, funeral, send off, or burying (whatever you call it), how do you want people to speak about your life? No really, think about it, and then record your thoughts.

Buckler Up

September 2
Proverbs 2

"He stores up sound wisdom for the upright; He is a shield to those who walk in integrity." Proverbs 2:7, NASB

"After these things the word of the Lord came to Abram in a vision, saying, 'Do not fear, Abram, I am a shield to you; your reward shall be very great.'" Genesis 15:1, NASB

"How blessed is the man whose strength is in You, in whose heart are the highways to Zion! Passing through the valley of Baca they make it a spring; the early rain also covers it with blessings. They go from strength to

strength, every one of them appears before God in Zion. O Lord God of hosts, hear my prayer; give ear, O God of Jacob! Selah. Behold our shield, O God, and look upon the face of Your anointed. For a day in Your courts is better than a thousand outside. I would rather stand at the threshold of the house of my God than dwell in the tents of wickedness. For the Lord God is a sun and shield; the Lord gives grace and glory; no good thing does He withhold from those who walk uprightly. O Lord of hosts, how blessed is the man who trusts in You! Psalms 84:5-12, NASB

There is nothing like being baptized in the confidence of God's blessing! It's a total immersion in His presence, forging ahead in life, no matter the circumstances. It's not always a given, but when those winds of refreshment really blow across our fatigue-drenched spirits, they give us life! The Holy Spirit always seems to know when we need Him the most!

What a wonderful and caring Father we have!

Today's voice of Wisdom reminds us of an important promise:

"He is a shield to those who walk in integrity."

The word for "shield" is a military term meaning "protector or buckler." It's a defensive apparatus that can be helpful in preventing damage to the major organs of a man's body.

True enough, one might lose a limb or be gashed and pummeled elsewhere on his body, but in those days, the shield was the most effective in protecting against arrows and swords entering a man's body cavity. Wisdom declares that a man suited in his integrity has the Lord for his shield. True enough, life deals its wounding blows, but the Lord has promised a vested interest in protecting and defending us when integrity is our life expression.

The Psalmist in today's text mentions the Valley of Baca (the valley of the weepers, the place of tombs). Part of that promise of having His shield is to make even the hard things in our lives a source of our strength, renewal, and refreshment.

In other words, we don't have to live in dry bitterness. He will come, even in the pain and hurt, and bring us unexpected life in places where we only see death.

A shield He is. A shield He will be!

In The Pages

How often do you see immediate payback or "fruit" for integrity? Ever notice how people who don't live by integrity are slightly confused when they see integrity? What does that tell you about the normal levels of hope in peoples' hearts?

Second half of life people are probably more thankful for how they've been protected (without always knowing it) rather than strutting around in confidence of some kind of supernatural kevlar. Grace allows us to accept whatever today brings, and sometimes, today brings pain, heartache, loss, and grief. The love that God has for his people cannot be thwarted or measured in terms of our seasons of suffering. Life is good, but it can be hard. Blessed be the name of the Lord! —MDP 2018

Hanging on a Hinge

September 3
Proverbs 3

"Surely he scorneth the scorners: but he giveth grace unto the lowly." Proverbs 3:34, KJV

Today's verse is part of a nine-verse package (verses 27-35) outlining five basic principles for relationships. All of the more modern translations use the word *"mock"* instead of *"scorneth."*

The basic idea is that we reap what we sow. We can't hear this enough! There is something terribly dreadful in the thought that God is capable and willing to give us back the crap we dish out.

Considering the fact that Patti and I live and work in a discipleship-oriented spiritual culture, I'm all about this stuff, and you should be too! Extremely passionate young men and women, who are very serious about their walk with God, surround us on a daily basis. I rarely question their motives. It's their limited vision I question, hampered by their lack of life experience.

I frequently hear grandiose declarations and selfish complaints that I know are going to birth nasty fruit. There are too many bold words and not enough silent restraints. Even though the "lowly" mentioned here includes the poor and afflicted, it also means *"the humble."*

Discipleship doesn't develop naturally without generous doses of humility along the way. It's really the hinge upon which this kind of spiritual growth hangs. Can the learner, student, disciple, son or daughter be humble enough to place his or her self under authority?

It's the biggest question that hangs in the balance of real discipleship.

In the discipleship arena, the "scorner" or "mocker" is the person who says, "I just need God. No man can give me what I need!" Sadly, I've heard this one before. It sounds fairly spiritual and overly religious, but it's contrary to the basic discipleship principles that Jesus lived out and the apostles taught.

"You younger men, likewise, be subject to your elders; and all of you, clothe yourselves with humility toward one another, for God is opposed to the proud, but gives grace to the humble. Therefore humble yourselves under the mighty hand of God, that He may exalt you at the proper time, casting all your anxiety on Him, because He cares for you" (1 Peter 5:5-7, NASB).

Holy-frik, Batman! This is serious business here! Don't be mistaken; this isn't just a guideline for males. Young men and women alike need to hear this . . . like, deep inside of their heart!

Then, at the *"proper time,"* His time, the appointed right time, He'll exalt, promote, commission, and under-gird a lifetime of service in the Kingdom! But prideful insolence towards authority and the discipleship process only brings heartbreaking frustration and prolonged repetition in very small and confined places.

The promise is that "he gives grace unto the lowly". Supernatural provision! And He gives us more than enough for every situation we'll ever face!

Now, is your authority trustworthy? That is a completely different discussion.

In The Pages

How respectful have you been to spiritual authority? Have you said the words, *"I need your cover, help, or love in my life"* to men or women who are spiritual leaders? What is the biggest drawback in your submission to authority? What does that say about your need to submit anyway?

He Ain't Budging

September 4
Proverbs 4

"Keep your heart with all diligence, for out of it spring the issues of life." Proverbs 4:23, NKJV

This is one of those loadstone verses that will continually bridge together all of time. It will forever be both ancient and contemporary. I mean, if this verse isn't true, then what's the point?

It was as fresh on Jesus' lips as it was on Solomon's. It really didn't seem to matter to Jesus what kind of nonsense you might spout around Him, He always brought you back to a place of heart examination.

As zealous as the Pharisees were, Jesus never let them forget this important aspect of relating to God. He drove them nuts with this stuff:

"You brood of vipers, how can you, being evil, speak what is good? For the mouth speaks out of that which fills the heart" (Matthew 12:34, NASB).

So what do you think? Do you think Jesus had issues with their words, or their hearts? Do you think He judged them based on their speech, or was there a deeper problem? I mean... He called them vipers! He probably had bigger issues with what filled those guys, rather than the actual words that came out of their mouths.

Pharisees were very careful not to say anything that would defile them, so the "poison" (problem) was in their heart (mind, emotions, and overall value system). Their "viper-ness" was the problem, not necessarily the stuff they preached.

This is hard for us, because westernized Christians have learned how to do and say all the right things in our religious belonging systems. We can really put on a good show of how it's supposed to be done, and our religious performances really aren't helping anyone.

**Take it from this old country boy—
Jesus ain't budging on this heart thing.**

I'm pretty sure He yawns at all those words and activities coming from less-than-right hearts. As the Oracle told Neo in The Matrix, "I thought you'd have all that figured out by now."[3] Nope, not yet.

The lesson for today (and every day) is so simple . . . yet most difficult:

Keep your heart.

What does that mean? How do we do that? Can we do that?

It takes great effort (and awareness) to be responsible for the stuff that's in your heart. That is why Wisdom and the God Incarnate make such a big deal about it.

Strong's Concordance says the word "keep" is **nâtsar** (pronounced naw-tsar′), meaning "to guard, in a good sense (to protect, maintain, obey, etc.)." The NASB translates the verse as, "Watch over your heart."

We need to pay close attention to what's really important here. We get so easily lost in all of life's distractions, along with religious externals. Autopilot is not going to work on this issue.

Our heart is our center.

As our heart goes, our lives go. We need some of what David had: *"Put me on trial, Lord, and cross-examine me. Test my motives and my heart"* (Psalms 26:2, NLT).

It's such a dangerously taxing prayer. But it is the right prayer.

In The Pages

When was the last time you prayed Psalms 139:23-24? After you prayed, did you wait around for a response? What did He say to you? If it's been a while since you put your heart out there, how about taking some time to dial in again for His download. He appreciates the sincere effort.

Beautiful Bordeaux

September 5
Proverbs 5

"He will die for lack of instruction, and in the greatness of his folly he will go astray." Proverbs 5:23, NASB

In the first nine chapters of Proverbs, Solomon expounds on sexual impropriety five different times. Today's verse is part of a three-verse package that closes out chapter five. Personally, this may be one of my favorite chapters in Proverbs.

The King's passion pours like beautiful Bordeaux. The whole chapter is wonderfully crafted to remind us again of the purity, and exhilaration, of sanctified sexuality.

There is nothing to hide, nothing to be ashamed of. The covenant love between a man and woman is some of God's best creative work! Even if you're single, you can appreciate the sensitive dialogue, preparing you for a day when you will engage in love duly consummated in marital wonder!

There are times when Solomon brings highly caustic warnings about the things he wants us to avoid. We should appreciate the "heads up," whether we're involved in that stuff or not. Today's text is the kind of warning I'm referring to. In fact, let's take a look at that whole three-verse package I mentioned earlier:

For the ways of a man are before the eyes of the Lord, and He watches all his paths. His own iniquities will capture the wicked, and he will be held with the cords of his sin. He will die for lack of instruction, and in the greatness of his folly he will go astray (Proverbs 5:21-23, NASB).

Part of Solomon's desire was to take away our excuses. He didn't want us victimized by our own ignorance and shortsightedness. So he tells us what we're up against if we decide to live disorderly and cast aside our sacred vows.

Again, I firmly believe Solomon was at his best when he *went there* with these sensitive topics. He had his own fair share of rough patches, made some less-than-wise decisions, and it was still fresh in his memory (1 Kings 11:3-6).

So what does Solomon do here?

He paints some serious imagery! It's brilliant, really! The first thing he says is that God sees everything we do. Quite frankly, that's got the potential to be some scary shit right there. It kind of depends on what you've got going on.

Next, Solomon tells us how God scrutinizes, studies, and thinks about our paths and decisions (no less startling). Then, the heart of Wisdom says there are ropes and chains of bondage that follow the ways of the wicked. Sin has consequences, and if you've paid any attention to life already, you know this is a solid truth.

Today's verse, the last verse of the chapter, reminds us that if we get lax in discipline and ignore all the safeguards and privileges of covenant, we can expect those precious things we possess to shrivel and die. The courts do not finalize divorce. That happens long before, because couples wander away from the healthy mechanisms that hold secure love in place.

Years of folly and too many seasons of neglect lead to droughts that choke the life out of love. Let's commit to something different, no matter the cost. It's worth it.

In The Pages

Marriages fail all the time for various reasons. The ones you've seen struggle or dissolve, what was the real problem? Think about your marriage or the marriage you hope to have in the future. What safeguards need to be in place to ensure healthy attention to your mate and to prevent your own drifts of emotional isolation? If you're divorced, the love of God has not been forfeited! How healed is your heart now?

Hot Mess

September 6
Proverbs 6

"Can a man scoop a flame into his lap and not have his clothes catch on fire? Can he walk on hot coals and not blister his feet? So it is with the man who sleeps with another man's wife. He who embraces her will not go unpunished. Excuses might be found for a thief who steals because he is starving. But if he is caught, he must pay back seven times what he stole, even if he has to sell everything in his house. But the man who commits adultery is an utter fool, for he destroys himself. He will be wounded and disgraced. His shame will never be erased. For the woman's jealous

husband will be furious, and he will show no mercy when he takes revenge. He will accept no compensation, nor be satisfied with a payoff of any size." Proverbs 6:27-35, NLT

This is frikk'n brutal! I've poured over these verses all morning and I can't find any silver lining. It's so . . . naked and "out there."

It's not about condemnation or shaming anyone. It's just simple and uncompromising truth. There are dire consequences to "fooling around" with another man's wife or another woman's husband.

Although the consequences mentioned here are significant, what really sticks out is the fact that whoever plays this dangerous game has no justification whatsoever that warrants the infidelity. Let that sink in. No warranted justification! NONE!

Whatever voodoo web the devil helped you spin in your mind to justify what you're doing is wrong. It falsely gives you permission to even speculate what it would be like to touch what is forbidden. Before the gun even sounds, you're already disqualified from running in this race. There is no exception.

The breach against sacred covenant is never healthy for anyone involved. Make no mistake the consequences are expensive and lasting. Wisdom paints a gruesome picture for those who commit such crimes against covenant.

The first two questions set the tone. The appeal is to basic instinct and sensibility, regardless of age.

One of the very first lessons we're taught is that fire burns. We say to babies and toddlers, *"Hot! No, no! Hot! That will hurt, baby!"* We make a big deal about the fireplace or the kitchen oven, all because we don't want them getting burned or, even worse, scarred.

Momma Wisdom is doing the same thing here. If you play with this fire, you're going to get burned. Simple wisdom.

As many times as I've read these warnings, I've never once been offended or felt judged by Wisdom's harshness. Frankly, I have felt very loved and cared for. I have sensed a covering desire from the Lord's heart to reverence and steward the legitimate love that He has provided for me. That's what we're supposed to take away from all of this.

Legitimate is real love. Illegitimate only gets you burned and leaves you with a hot mess.

In The Pages

Have you learned to relate to the Lord's heart through reading wisdom literature, or are you just concerned with "keeping the rules?" Which of those two would you suspect He'd most want you to benefit from? Are you thankful for wisdom's invasive tactics? Why, or why not?

Staying Out of the "Goo"

September 7
Proverbs 7

"Now therefore, listen to me, my children; pay attention to the words of my mouth: do not let your heart turn aside to her ways, do not stray into her paths" Proverbs 7:24-25, NKJV

When I was very young (probably about 10 years old), my grandfather had a single-shot .410 shotgun that he let me carry for him whenever we hunted dove together. I was a pretty good shot, and he was always amazed that I could bring down game with that little gun.

The first season I actually got to carry my own gun, he'd stand right behind me, watching every move I made. It was a constant barrage of instructions and gun safety reminders.

Over and over again he'd bark, *"Is your safety on? Where is your gun pointed? Is the safety on? Don't put that gun on your shoulder! Is the safety on? Get your finger off that trigger. How do we cross a fence with guns? Is the safety on? Point that gun up or at the ground. Is the safety on?"*

It was constant chatter, and I do mean constant! Then afterwards, while we were cleaning birds and our hands were covered in bird "goo," he'd make up some crap about how he'd witnessed some friend, or a guy he'd hunted with, blow off his foot, hand, or some other various appendages because he had mishandled his gun. I always suspected it was a big load of donkey dung, but when your hands are covered with bird innards, it can make quite an impression on you.

I rarely handle a gun now where I don't hear my grandfather's voice drilling me with his incessant coaching. And that was a really long time ago!

Proverbs 7 reads like an enthralling mini-drama that takes you through the dangers of adultery! Every time you read it, there she is again, the adulteress, peeking through the window, just waiting to pounce on the innocent, the gullible, and most assuredly, the dumb.

Just because you've read it all before doesn't mean you're exempt from what is being revealed here. You need to feel this every time you read it. It needs to disturb you, make you uncomfortable.

The potential destruction, the lasting peril of this kind of personal failure, has the devil's invite to ruin your life, jack up your family, and destroy the heart of the person who gave you his or her pledge. So, whether you're single or happily married, pay attention to the details of this story.

Let Wisdom's voice lovingly annoy you. Invite her counsel and hear once more: *This is dangerous business. Pay attention. You're not exempt. Be aware and use caution!*

Honestly, when you're 10-years old, it's hard to appreciate discipline's repetitious instruction. But once you've reached some measure of maturity, you shouldn't have to have your hands in the "goo" before you realize you should have listened.

Could we just live wisely and spare ourselves the mess?

In The Pages

Did you read the whole chapter again? What struck a chord with you that you haven't seen or heard before? What kind of "goo" have you had your hands in?

Deny the Wuss

September 8
Proverbs 8

"To you, O men, I call, and my voice is to the sons of men." Proverbs 8:4, NASB

"All human nature vigorously resist grace, because grace changes us and change is painful." Flannery O'Connor

I love this verse in the NASB translation! It reeks of authority and prophetic thunder. It rattles the bones and clears the head.

Wisdom is speaking and placing a demand on her sons and daughters to hear and respond to her voice. It roars in tones of excellence. She calls for something much more than floating downstream.

I included this quote from Flannery O'Connor because I feel it puts a finger on why people resist doing hard stuff. We don't want to swim upstream. We usually won't challenge ourselves without some sort of external pressure.

Just as grace changes us (and by that, I mean the real essence of supernatural power, not just slick acrostics and religious slogans), Lady Wisdom's voice has the power to impact us deeply. When we win internal battles that deny the "wussy" in us, it stimulates confidence, sweet victory, and savory enjoyment.

To know you've said "yes" to pain and that "hard" didn't kill you is one of the most satisfying realizations in life! Sometimes, overcoming "hard" is what makes things truly great!

Rarely does Wisdom come with soft, gentle fade-a-ways. Instead she says, *"Hey! I know what you're thinking, and that's a bad idea. There is another way to approach this. Together, we can do better. Let's do better!"*

My parents used to do that to me when I was a kid. My wife does it to me now. She'll say, *"That look on your face isn't good. Michael Dean, what kind of trouble are you stirring up? Straighten up."* Frik! That's not much of a poker face.

One of the premier values of healthy spiritual community is the willingness to call each other out. Let me be clear here, it's not just about establishing the pecking order or identifying sin. I'm referring to our prophetic responsibility to lean into each other with a jealous desire for each other's betterment!

Hey! Time to rise up to another level.

Time to stop fooling around.

Time to shift the gears and climb, baby. Climb!

Eagles soar. YOU are an eagle!

Stop hopping around here like a frog.

Whether it's received as a rebuke, edification, or encouragement, we have a genuine responsibility to one another to declare a hopeful destiny and point to greatness. THAT is what we can take away from today's scripture.

Wisdom calls! She forces us to acknowledge our sloppy discontentment and to face the discomfort of discipline, which polishes our character. What a gift her call is to us all!

In The Pages

Who tells you the truth about *you*? Can you be "called out," and truly receive it with thankfulness? Can you say "thank you," and mean it? Who do *you* need to call out?

Vacuum of Modesty

September 9
Proverbs 9

"A foolish and bold woman who knows not modesty, comes to want a morsel. She sits at the doors of her house, on a seat openly in the streets, calling to passers by, and to those that are going right on their ways." Proverbs 9:13-15, Brenton LXX English

MODESTY.

Now there is a word you don't hear anymore.

The game has changed drastically in the past 100 years. It used to be a virtue. Now it's like an impediment.

Maybe it's not all *her* fault. I've touched on this before. With the seeming evaporation of masculine prowess (especially in spiritual culture) and the heightened expansion of feminine energy across the board, it appears that, in order for a woman (especially a single woman) to be noticed by a man, she has to be anything but modest.

It seems we've lost all respect for healthy boundaries, discretion, and the allure of mystery. Sampling the treats at Sam's Club is one thing, but the free give-a-ways prior to marriage is not helpful to the overall strength of continuing covenant.

"All things are permissible" (1 Corinthians 10:23)

YES, God loves you regardless of what you've done, what you do, or whether you know it or not.

"But, not all things are profitable." (1 Corinthians 10:23)

You had better believe it! You wouldn't commit a murder believing it's ok because God has forgiven you already. It doesn't work like that. God's love doesn't grant us the "go ahead" to be douche bags.

His love will be with you always, no matter what, but your actions could also mean your incarceration in a penal institution. We are responsible for how we steward the freedoms we've been granted. Wisdom suggests another approach to the woman depicted here today.

This failed attention to discretion that has this woman "all out" in the streets calling everyone's attention to herself is what puts Wisdom's voice on edge. This is not how she was created to be.

She is not at peace; she is not attending to her duties. She has forsaken all else to do the thing *she* wants to do. The whole scenario feels lost, desperate, and empty.

She's loud, barking orders, disturbing the lives of passers-by, and engrossed in their daily duties. This isn't the woman described in Proverbs 31. None of those things apply here.

Do I sound chauvinistic? Maybe I am. But honestly, there is nothing more confusing and out-of-sorts with what seems normal than a pushy woman who has lost her sense of what really makes her beautiful and charming.

Violence in her spirit is not charming or beautiful. It's one thing for her to rise up to defend and protect at any given moment. It's quite another to be a regular brawler in word and attitude.

Granted, I'm older, white, southern, and probably biased because I've lived the past 55 plus years around very feminine women. They're plenty strong, exotically beautiful, but mysteriously complex. They've taught me much about the power of a modest woman.

In The Pages

Does a strong woman have to be brash and mouthy? Does a woman have to dismiss modesty or decency in order to be appealing today?

The same things could just as easily be asked of a man. Does a man have to be brash and mouthy to be manly? Times are changing. The days of men who have no respect for the rights of anyone or anything but themselves are over. The tolerance of our culture for men who exercise privilege and power for their own desires or advantage has run its course... and not a second too soon! —MDP 2018

Falling Towers of Entitlement

September 10
Proverbs 10

"The proverbs of Solomon: a wise child brings joy to a father; a foolish child brings grief to a mother. Tainted wealth has no lasting value, but right living can save your life. The Lord will not let the godly go hungry, but he refuses to satisfy the craving of the wicked. Lazy people are soon poor; hard workers get rich." Proverbs 10:1-4, NLT

One of the most rewarding things about living in the second half of life is that you're less devastated when things don't work out according to plan. Sometimes, a promise is nothing more than a stall, and a verbal (or written) commitment that just isn't going to happen.

I've learned that part of the beauty of raising children is in helping them to establish boundaries and foundations of security. Even though they don't always appreciate it, it's good for their developing self-esteem to believe they can do anything, they are the best, the most beautiful, *numero uno*, and the ultimate beloved of mommy and daddy. We need that kind of stuff when we're growing up!

But when you're 65 years old (heck, even 35 or 25 years old!), it's time to stop going through life with that kind of ego need.

I frequently read in social media, *"God is sooooo gooooood because . . . [fill in the blank]."* Nothing wrong with giving God a shout out for a blessing! Let's be clear about that.

But if they hadn't gotten what they wanted, is God still good anyway?

Was this something this person has been praying about for a long time, maybe even felt entitled to for whatever reason? Because they've been "good," worked hard, and followed the rules?

God is not Santa, the Easter Bunny, or the frikk'n Tooth Fairy. You're not 9-years-old anymore. You're not exempt from getting hammered just because you told the truth. It's time for those kinds of ego-driven entitlement towers to be knocked down. And (thank you God!) they do fall! All the time!

My point here is not to prove Solomon wrong.

Not the point at all! I do believe the scripture to be extremely helpful when handled properly. But our ego-charged perspectives are so jacked up. We're easily confused by today's text. We read it as black and white, right or wrong, win or lose—the good guys (us) always win.

Sometimes the *"godly" do* go hungry, and not all lard-ass *lazy* people are poor. This might be a real shocker to you, but there are lots of hard-working people on this planet who are not financially wealthy! What? Not every player gets a trophy? Another tower falls!

The old containers of formulistic discipline are good and necessary when you're young in your mind and innocent in your spirit. But when it's time to grow up and push away from that familiar table of absolutes, you're going to have to accept the fact that life can be very hard at times despite our best efforts.

There may be some towers of entitlement in your psyche that need to come tumbling down. It's called: growing-the-frik-up!

Part of growing up is coming to appreciate the foundations as the starting point. You don't play guitar like Stevie Ray Vaughan first time you pick it up. You learn chords, timing, licks, and rifts. Once the foundations are laid (after many years of discipline), all that creative expression is then free to explore and exploit the exceptions to the rules. Color moves into your brave new world, and you see it for how it really is... fallen towers and all!

In The Pages

How well do you deal with disappointment? Can you make room for God's silence or alterations, or do you have to have your expectations met, no matter the cost to you or others around you? Do you know God, or do you know *about* God?

Living On The Upside

September 11
Proverbs 11

"Though hand join in hand, the wicked shall not be unpunished: but the seed of the righteous shall be delivered." Proverbs 11:21, KJV

"Count on this: The wicked won't get off scot-free, and God's loyal people will triumph. Proverbs 11:21, MSG

911. Three numbers forever fused together. Before 2001, 9-1-1 could have meant any number of things. Now, it means only one thing... a nightmare!

The only other date in American history to parallel the horror of 911 would probably be December 7, 1941: the bombing of Pearl Harbor. President Roosevelt prophesied, *"A date which will live in infamy."* What 911 means to us is just as significant, if not more. The pain is still very real.

On a recent trip to New York City (2012), Patti and I had the opportunity to visit the 911 Memorial. It was a very spiritual experience, walking around those magnificent pools, reading the names of the innocent victims and the heroes, and admiring the simple beauty of it all. There is both beauty and sorrow at Ground Zero.

At one point, I remember looking up at the new World Trade Center (under construction) stretching upward to fill its rightful place in that beautiful NYC skyline, and I thought: *mankind has the ability to create some amazing things!* A quick glance back down to the memorial, the counter-punch came: *as skilled as we are, evil can be just as creative to tear down and destroy what we have built.*

As good and well intentioned as most people are, we live in a fallen world. We share space with people who are just as strongly committed to evil, primarily death and destruction. When I read Wisdom's thoughts in today's text, it's clear that she sees those differences in us also.

Simple question: How do you want to utilize the rest of your life?

Do you want to be a part of the "building up" or the "tearing down?" This question applies to anything you have going on in your little world. It's important for us to take this question seriously, because the Lord definitely sees the difference. So, here's some food for thought:

Speech: Are you speaking positively? Pouring life into others? Or are you the "Debbie Downer" of the group? Do you always have to point out the negative? Are you encouraging, or do you keep quiet when someone does well because you are jealous?

Service: Can you give to others without expecting something in return, or do you keep record?

Relationships: How many "real friends" do you have? How much emotional weight do you carry in the relationship? Are you doing your share? Are you loyal?

Marriage: When is the last time you looked into the eyes of your spouse and said the words, *I love you*? If you can't remember, it's been way too long. If you know what's keeping you from saying those words, why not remove the blockage?

God: Are you growing in your dependence upon the Lord? Do you live spiritually or religiously? When is the last time you asked the Lord for His insight and direction for a specific issue you're dealing with? Are you satisfied with what you've experienced and given away in His name? Do you bear and shine forth His light while exerting a positive existence? The world desperately needs this kind of person!

In The Pages

Take some time to journal the above questions. It's a great day to be fully alive and totally grateful!

Juice of Contrast

September 12
Proverbs 12

"The thoughts of the righteous are right: but the counsels of the wicked are deceit. The words of the wicked are to lie in wait for blood: but the mouth of the upright shall deliver them. The wicked are overthrown, and are not: but the house of the righteous shall stand." Proverbs 12:5-7, KJV

Do you ever wonder where this "juice" comes from that Solomon used to lay down all these Proverbs? *How* he laid it out? *Where* he laid it out? We know he asked for Wisdom, and the Lord gave him a serious download, but how did he formulate all those thought patterns into such applicable portions?

I believe he was inspired by daily life. When I was a denominational senior pastor, everyday life taught me which things needed to be addressed. Sheep get all kinds of external parasites, and sometimes these issues have to be addressed to the entire Body.

As pastors, the things we see and hear among our sheep heavily affect us. Of course, it takes a download from the Holy Spirit to "package it" the right way, where it will fall on listening hearts. Anyway, when I read today's text, I realize Solomon must have had a few up-close and personal encounters with some less-than-honorable characters.

I think Jesus drank from that same juice.

Jesus could go "radar" on you in a heartbeat. He could "read your mail," so to speak, along with just about everyone else's mail He came in contact with.

He knew the traditions of men. He understood the concerns of society. He saw need everywhere, and He always knew what was going on inside of the people he met:

"But Jesus, on His part, was not entrusting Himself to them for He knew all

men" (John 2:24).

He wasn't moved or swayed by the strong winds of culture or man's agendas.

In his great sermon on the mountainside, Jesus continually said, *"You have heard."* Then He would counteract whatever it was they had *heard* they should do, with what God says they should do (Matthew 5:21, 27, 33, 38, 43). His experience on Earth handed Him broken pieces of pottery than needed the Master's hand. Then He would speak, the fog would lift, and the brilliance of His simple clarity would shine forth like the sun.

Today's Proverb contrasts the hearts of the righteous and the wicked. Justice opposes deceit. Edifying speech counteracts words that kill. And the certainty of lasting impact stands against the fragility of evil's abode.

There is a big difference between the righteous and the wicked, and Wisdom wants to make sure we see it. What is righteous is not always how man has been taught by society to operate.

May we all be filled with His juice!

"You have heard." Yes, Lord, we've seen and heard.

In The Pages

In what areas of your life has the Lord given you specific instructions on how to live differently from the norm? Did you obey in the moment, or has it become a permanent adjustment in your life? How often do you notice the differences between Jesus' instructions and "conventional wisdom" in today's culture?

The Heart Behind The Heat

September 13
Proverbs 13

"He who ignores discipline comes to poverty and shame, but whoever heeds correction is honored." Proverbs 13:18, NIV

Check out the lyrics to an incredible song by my friends:

INTIMACY
Jonathan & Melissa Helser
Used by permission

These hands You made to hold yours, my love
These feet You shaped to walk with you in our garden
These eyes You placed to gaze upon your face
These lips You formed to kiss my Beloved

I was made, I was made, for intimacy

These ears You made to hear your rhythm of love
This voice You placed to sing songs of grace
This hair You wove, you numbered every strand
This gaze You love, it captures you with a glance

I was made, I was made, for intimacy

If your perspectives in life were shaped by these lyrics, would it change how you read today's Proverb? I suspect I know your answer.

I'm guilty of this myself sometimes, but I think we read wisdom and forget the heart behind the voice. Although we need safe boundaries and rigid pushback from strong containers early on in our lives, we also need to be developing a heightened awareness of what's behind the discipline.

Military drill sergeants break down new recruits in order to bring them to a place of unwavering obedience to the chain of command. Supposedly, this is so the recruit will carry out orders, no matter what. There can't be a debate on every detail of instruction. In the middle of a fire-fight would be a bad time to question operational objectives.

Those nasty drill sergeants do what they do because they're trying to save the lives of those they're responsible for and build trust among the soldiers. As rough as it is, it has more to do with building character and promoting a unit of honor, than any sort of morbid fascination with pain.

If you're a leader who lost a man or two because he mishandled his rifle, you might be pretty passionate about gun safety. But if you can't see the big picture, if you don't understand the care and concern behind all of those pressured details, you'll stiff-arm your commanding officer, therefore sabotaging your own growth and development and putting the people alongside you at risk. Yeah, that's why you get a boot up the tailpipe when you're not dialed in and paying attention.

The heart behind the heat is honor, intimacy, and love. If we don't understand that, it feels like a nightmare. But if we can get over ourselves, it's much better to lean into the resistance that discipline offers us. It will only strengthen our resolve and tone our abilities to carry out the objectives of Kingdom living!

In The Pages

Where do you need the most discipline in your life? Are you avoiding resistance, or are you looking for ways to lean into an unmovable container? Having a partner to develop discipline helps. Who could benefit from the same discipline as you?

Chillin' On Momma

September 14
Proverbs 14

"Wisdom rests in the heart of one who has understanding, but in the hearts of fools it is made known." Proverbs 14:33, NASB

As I have tackled this writing project, my approach has been to write only one devotional each day. Every day I write from the chapter that correlates to the date, and then I assign the months in a less strategic order. Today's entry is the 12th devo I've written for the 14th day, so this is it for Proverbs 14.

I'm telling you this because I feel I've been treated well by the Holy Spirit, and I feel genuinely blessed to touch on this particular verse today. There is no telling how many times I have read this verse, but today I really dug into it, and I got some of the most satisfying imagery I could have ever hoped for. Such a rich and delightful discovery, it makes my heart smile! I pray it does the same for you.

Like the perfect piece of cheesecake, let's start at the crispy, buttery back and work towards the creamy point. In Keil and Delitzsch's *Commentary on the Old Testament*, they rightly assert, *"Most interpreters know not what to make out of the second line here."* They're right—it's thin in most commentaries.

What we *do* know is that whatever is going on inside the *heart of the fool* is in contrast to what's happening inside the *heart of one who has understanding*. So I guess we need to nibble at the point after all.

"Wisdom rests..." And here is where the treasure lay. The word for *"rests"* is **nûwach** (pronounced *noo'-akh*), which means *"to settle down, to dwell, to stay, to withdraw and give comfort."*

There is a great passage where David connects the dots beautifully,

"Surely I have composed and quieted my soul; like a weaned child rests against his mother, my soul is like a weaned child within me" (Psalms 131:2, NASB).

As David would sit in the presence of God with his instrument, we can hear his soothing melody and feel the warmth of the Lord's presence and peaceful truth.

"Wisdom rests in the heart..." As a baby that has long suckled at mommy's breast, now weaned and satisfied in an overflow of nourishment and *rest*, the babe leans back into what has sustained his or her life. What trust! What security and assured contentment!

Nothing has to be proved.

Rest is right here and now. Composure and quiet take over.

There may not be a more needed message to the "under 65" crowd for life!

With the *fool* (the one who will not or does not understand) there is little allowance for *rest*. His own insecurities demand that he prove what little he knows.

The *"it"* of today's Proverb is a shallow exposition that may temporarily impress, but cannot be maintained long term. Whatever puddles of truth he possesses just don't go that deep. Some steps were missed along the way. The love marinade of Wisdom's slow roast was prematurely interrupted.

To be "belly full" of Wisdom comes with an understanding that *rest* and quiet are good. Fools have yet to figure all that out. May the

Lord grant us the peace of Wisdom's great *rest*, deep inside our *heart*.

In the Pages

Have you ever been around someone who has wanted to impress you with his or her wisdom? How long did it take you to figure out that the words didn't match the advertisements? How inclined were you to follow that person, regardless of what was promised?

Soul Sick

September 15
Proverbs 15

"He that refuseth instruction despiseth his own soul: but he that heareth reproof getteth understanding." Proverbs 15:32, KJV

Frik! It's all over the news today... another mass shooting in America! (2012)

Innocent people doing innocent things, now the victim of someone's sick rage. I don't know if you've noticed or not, but we have serious issues on this planet. Quite honestly, we are not a happy world.

As ineffective as the "Church" is (*and I'm sure if you're stuck in some sort of religious "ism" where you think your way is the only way, I probably just offended you*), it (the Church) still does a decent job of *speaking* God's truth about His real, tangible, unconditional love.

Heck, even the Beatles did their part. Songwriters, poets, and screenplays all continue to broadcast the world's desperation for love. But we don't seem to be getting the message as a whole.

Yes, isolated occurrences of love do happen, and it's the bomb-diggity when they do. But wow... there are times when it looks like darkness is eating light for lunch.

I don't know any other way to put it: I think we are soul-sick.

Yes, even the Church. I wish I could say the Church has stronger marriages. I wish we could believe the world's sexual misappropriations were only an "out there" issue.

Addictions, compulsions, hate, jealousy, selfish ambition, and all other demonic influences are just as prevalent inside the Church's walls as they are out in the streets.

Ok, so now I've really offended you. But think about what I'm saying. We are soul-sick primarily because we despise and hate ourselves. Self-hate is a serious problem on our globe. It only gets worse when we hate others more than we hate ourselves.

Go to the mall, go to school, or go to a church and watch the people. Really watch and see if you don't conclude the same thing. People *"despiseth"* their souls and hate themselves. New clothes, more plastic, and whiter teeth won't fix any of your problems. The manifestation of self-hate in our society is killing us . . . literally.

It's all rooted in the spirit of rejection. Self-hate has convinced us to change our look, change our weight, or change our overall appearance in order to be loved and to rightly love ourselves, and others.

These changes for health reasons is one thing.
Change for acceptance is quite another.

Honestly, I don't think that approach is working too well for us. We need something else to happen... something more lasting.

Paul wrote, *"So faith comes from hearing, and hearing by the word of Christ"* (Romans 10:17, NASB).

Somehow, someway, the truth of God's absolute **unconditional love** has got to hit the hearts of people on this orb. How we've been doing it doesn't seem to be working.

People are wounded. They need to feel more loved, not more rejected. Those who can tolerate Christian paradigms need to be changed from the inside out. We need to apply what we know and touch others with the same love we've so graciously received.

The world needs it . . . badly!

Without His love consuming this planet, we're done for! But it can't just be our motto. We have to live it out! It has to be our daily lives! Until everyone really get it!

In The Pages

How well do you love on the people you live alongside? Do they know you love them without you telling them? What's something you can do to show them you love them?

Gusher

September 16
Proverbs 16

"Understanding is a fountain of life to those who have it, but folly brings punishment to fools." Proverbs 16:22, NIV

I have to confess, I am having so much fun today as I write this entry. I'm in the largest cigar lounge in Central Texas. What's even better, it's in my hometown! So it's the ultimate man-hang for a little God reflection!

This isn't my first rodeo here. It's one of my happy places. It's interesting what happens when you allow God to show his face in those kinds of environments.

The word for *"understanding"* in today's text is a little different from what we're used to it meaning. This kind of *understanding* is sort of like insider trading; the information has gone deep, so it ensures success. The kind of person who possesses such knowledge, the kind that gives people assurance, has the opportunity to be a source of spiritual vitality to people who need it.

Good stewardship of such a spiritual water supply means you are "on call" 24/7. You never know when God might want you to do a little gushing.

So I was in this same lounge a few nights ago. Actually, it was Valentine's Day, and the joint was empty. Patti wasn't in town with me, so it was the perfect opportunity for me to flop down on a big leather couch and fire one up. It was the ultimate escape from a busy week—just hanging out, enjoying my alone time.

A couple puffs on my CAO and a guy I'd never seen in here before walks in with his wife. They nestled into a couple couches over with a couple of cigars and a nice bottle of champagne.

After a while, the guy starts engaging me in small talk. Honestly, I was kind of annoyed and sort of wished he would just shut up. He should have been lovin' on his woman so I could get back to lovin' on my stogie!

His name was Sherman. After a few minutes of small talk, he said, *"Man, who are you? There is something about you. Do I know you? What's the deal?"* I raised my eyebrows and thought, "Really dude, you want to go there right now?" Then he said, *"Are you a preacher or something?"* I guess the busted look was a dead-give-away.

Before I could respond, *"Would you come over and pray for my wife and I?"* I looked around to make sure we were still the only ones in the place, set my cigar down, and got up to walk over. As I slid onto the couch next to them, Sherman started crying! His wife threw her hands up in the air and started calling out Jesus' name. I placed my hands on Sherman's head and began to prophesy over him about his natural dad's love for him.

"Your dad is proud of you, Sherman. He loves you. You've done good, Sherman. You've done good!"

Come to find out, Sherman had buried his preacher dad about a year ago. He had serious doubts his dad was proud of him. He had been striving for a long time to get his dad's approval. It hurts your heart to see that kind of pain in a 57-year-old man.

He was pretty busted up. So my cigar went out. But God showed up! The deep fountain gushed. That is what fountains are designed to do! Our job is to let it happen, anywhere, at any time!

In the Pages

When is the last time you got caught up in an unexpected divine moment? Did you resist it, as I did, or did you oblige? Do you realize you have some serious stuff to give away?

Cruel Visitor

September 17
Proverbs 17

"A rebellious man seeks only evil, so a cruel messenger will be sent against him." Proverbs 17:11, NASB

"An evil man is bent only on rebellion; a merciless official will be sent against him." Proverbs 17:11, NIV

Either way you quote it, it's a forecast for trouble. Whether it's *"a rebellious man seeking only evil"* or *"an evil man bent on rebellion,"* it creates a vacuum for harsh retribution.

The word for "rebellion" is **merîy** (pronounced mer-ee´), which means "bitterness." It's from the root word **mârâh** (pronounced maw-raw´), also meaning "bitter (or unpleasant) to rebel, resist, provoking bitter change, being disobedient, or overall disobedience."

These are the same words we hear from an exasperated Moses,

"For I know your rebellion and your stubbornness; behold, while I am still alive with you today, you have been rebellious against the Lord; how much more, then, after my death" (Deuteronomy 31:27, NASB).

We hear something similar from a very agitated Samuel,

"For rebellion is as the sin of divination, and insubordination is as iniquity and idolatry. Because you have rejected the word of the Lord, He has also rejected you from being king" (1 Samuel 15:23, NASB).

That all happened a really long time ago, but I still pee myself just a little bit every time I read those passages. I think we need to cut below the first layer of skin and get into what's really happening under there.

Bitterness is in the *rebellion*.

It's the cause. Some "thing," some wound, some unforgivable deed, has led to deliberate disobedience. What might be scarier is that Father God actually takes it personally.

Saul thought he was just *rebelling* against the system, but he had actually stiff-armed the Lord. Samuel, in effect, was the *"cruel messenger,"* or *"merciless official."* He was the thorn under Saul's skin who told him the Lord had indeed regretted making Saul King over Israel (1 Samuel 15:26-35).

Let's face it... Saul was a jerk. I mean, a real tool. But I'm not willing to place all the blame on him. This whole *rebellion* thing, this demand for immediate satisfaction because of some unresolved bitterness, all began with the people.

Take a moment and read 1 Samuel 8:4-9. The problem was that Israel wanted a king *like all the other nations.* What they failed to realize was that they were being invited into a real relationship with Jehovah, who was not only their Lord, but who desperately desired for them to see Him as "Father."

They were bitter. They felt slighted, overlooked, not well cared for under the current situation. So God said, *Fine. They want a man king? I'll give them a king. But Samuel, you'll need to warn them what this is going to look like for them. If this is what they want, this is what they shall have. But this isn't going to be pretty* (1 Samuel 8:10-22).

Embittered *rebellion.* Let those words press on your heart. Embittered *rebellion.* Maybe it's time to stop forcing your own way with manipulation, controlling pressure, and little bitchy attitudes?

Wisdom says the *cruel messenger* (a special dispatch, angels, devils, prophets, teachers, or authority) has a little something for you. Unfortunately, they do make house calls.

In The Pages

What's on your mind right now? Is it your problem or someone else's? What are you going to do about it? How do you untangle from the webs of rebellion?

I'm at a different place from when I originally wrote this. I have no issue with the concept of cruel messengers that show up in our lives. But the rub comes when we believe that God is somehow punishing us. God doesn't have to punish us! WE punish US. We punish ourselves with our bitterness and outburst of self-focus. We create our own hell. We invite the emotional and relational torment when we really need to stop blaming God for the sour fruits that naturally grow around us because we planted bad seeds. — MDP / 2018

The Will To Live

September 18
Proverbs 18

"The will to live can get you through sickness, but no one can live with a broken spirit." Proverbs 18:14, YLT

"The human spirit can endure a sick body, but who can bear a crushed spirit?" Proverbs 18:14, NLT

*"I have seen the Spirit descending as a dove out of heaven, and He remained upon Him. I did not recognize Him, but He who sent me to baptize in water said to me, 'He upon whom you see the Spirit descending and remaining upon Him, this is the One who baptizes in the Holy Spirit.' I myself have seen, and have testified that **this is the Son of God**"* (John 1:32-34, NASB).

The same guy who said the above passage also sent his own followers to question Jesus:

"Are You the Expected One, or shall we look for someone else?"
Matthew 11:3, NASB

John was in a rough spot. This undomesticated wild man, who had stood for so long against the establishment in an effort to *"prepare the way"* for Jesus, had reached his breaking point. He was exhausted, alone, forgotten, and fully expecting an early exit.

He had known the answers to these questions since the day he danced in his momma's womb, but his spirit was failing. So he reached out. Somewhere deep inside, he craved a little bit of Wind. All he needed was a breath.

The stagnation in that dungeon was suffocating, and hope scurried away like the rats sharing his cell. *Come on Jesus! Help a brother out!*

Wisdom reminds us that *attitude* is a game changer.

The will to live, fight, and push back on the afflictions that pummel us, drastically affects our quality of life. Look around. Not everyone is fortunate enough to have his or her health. But there is something about a determined spirit that wills to take life by the horns and lead people to do the most amazing things.

I opened the newspaper this morning to see a picture of an 18-year-old kid who was born without fully developed arms or legs. He had been fitted to a special automobile, which allowed him to get where he needed to go without the help of another person.

The dude was Salutatorian of his high school and college-bound. He said, *"I can't afford depression. There is way too much life that needs to be lived."* So he pushes and forges his way into joy, grinning all the way! What an inspiration to us all!

Jesus didn't leave John or his followers hanging:

"Go and report to John what you hear and see: the blind receive sight and the lame walk, the lepers are cleansed and the deaf hear, the dead are raised up, and the poor have the gospel preached to them. And blessed is he who does not take offense at Me" (Matthew 11:4-6, NASB).

There is always hope if we can find the will to grab hold of some faith. I have to believe this was the Wind John was hoping for. Jesus knew what John needed before he even asked. So Jesus sent confirmation, which John took with him to the end.

In The Pages

Describe the person who has a *crushed spirit*. Who do you know who has made the choice to adjust his or her heart and attitude despite circumstances? Why not contact those people today and thank them for the inspiration they are to your faith?

Angels, Doobies, and other Freaky Stuff

September 19
Proverbs 19

"Many will seek the favor of a generous man, and every man is a friend to him who gives gifts." Proverbs 19:6, NASB

"Do not neglect to show hospitality to strangers, for by this some have entertained angels without knowing it." Hebrews 13:2, NASB

I have a picture in my mind of how this plays out. The *"generous"* or **nâdîyb** (pronounced *naw-deeb'*), is a prince or princess of nobility. Those who live among such people and benefit from their influence usually hold a generous person in great esteem and affection.

The generous have willing hearts and a liberal spirit. Wisdom says, *"many will seek their favor"*. Again, the Hebrew paints a picture.

Envision someone gently stroking the face of that prince or princess of nobility, out of sheer love, respect, and admiration. It comes from a genuine heart of thankfulness. Nobility has seen them and responded with kindness.

The great and wise King wrote, *"Do not withhold good from those to whom it is due, when it is in the power of your hand to do so"* (Proverbs 3:27, NKJV). This is a great reminder for Kingdom people!

We get so engrossed in our own complicated plans to please God that we forget the small faithful acts that really make an impact. Some people are so depleted in their faith even the simplest act of courtesy or kindness revives their hearts with hope!

Nothing messes with people like undeserved and unannounced acts of generosity! I just think Jesus is all about it!

Preacher people (that would be me) deal with all kinds of needs and hear all kinds of stories and pleas for financial help. Most requests are legit; some are not! People in need can learn how to work the system quickly. Having to decipher what's genuine and what's not can weigh heavily on your heart.

I get why churches deflect people to para-church ministries that specialize in feeding and clothing the poor. Having to make decisions about how much, and to whom, and for what cause, can be a wearisome cycle. We should have a great deal of respect for ministries out there that invite that kind of attention and fill those kinds of gaps!

Honestly, I think we get tested from time to time about these kinds of things. I know without a doubt, I've had angelic encounters. Some of those encounters were simply to get a message to me. Other times it was a simple wake-up call for me to check my sensitivity to a need.

I handed a guy a 20-dollar bill recently at a truck stop. He had asked for a dollar. You would have thought he had won the lottery. *"You're shittin' me?* (verbatim) *Really?"* I laughed, "Dude, it's no big deal." I meant it. He went to his truck, pulled up to the pump, got the gas he needed, and drove off.

Angel or not, his smile and awkward thanks were more than enough reward. But it's not always that easy.

I'm pretty sure that I unknowingly bought a destitute woman weed while in the Dominican Republic. Oh well. It still felt good to give to her. I remember thinking, *"Do angels get high?"* It's doubtful.

I advocate generosity. We can't police everyone's choices.

In The Pages

What kind of arguments do you have with yourself when approached for help by a stranger? Have you ever volunteered at a shelter, soup kitchen, or benevolence ministry? Would you pray about giving that a whirl?

Vapor Trails

September 20
Proverbs 20

"A righteous man who walks in his integrity— How blessed are his sons after him" Proverbs 20:7, NASB

The older I get, the weirder I get. What I mean by that is that I just don't have the time or energy to care about whether or not people "approve" of me anymore. Therefore, the real me is growing, and the false self is shrinking.

I'm not that familiar with my real *self* being so "out there" all the time, so I'm genuinely surprised by how weird I really am. Part of this whole self-discovery package includes finding out which things really move me.

For example, I am totally content to sit and watch my grandchildren play, eat, or whatever. Seriously, I can watch them watch *Toy Story* and be absolutely entertained.

Weird. I have also learned that I love the stories behind historical figures, especially when it comes to character development. Churchill had a story. Some of it was glorious, though most of it was unfortunate. Still, his story made him into the "Bulldog" the world needed at that particular time in history. See, it's weird.

I liked growing up in a small community. I learned early on that my parents' eyes were everywhere. I left my hometown at age 18, came back at 25, left again at 28, came back at 46, and left once more at 51.

We're in and out several times a year for family visits and pastoral responsibilities. It's always a pleasurable experience to be in town and run into people who know my parents or who have done business with my dad.

He had been in the insurance and real estate business for over 50 years. Although he had worked his tail off, his network of friends and associations is mind-blowing to me. The City Manager called my dad "Gentleman Joe." That's what I think about when I read today's proverb, *"how blessed are his sons after him"*.

Patti and I hear lots of stories. The people we disciple gradually let us into the rough stuff of their past. Although they have real desires to honor and bless their parents, not all have wide targets to aim for.

We're often reminded of how blessed we are to be able to walk freely in our old stomping grounds without concern of ridicule and scorn. My dad has always treated people with respect, served for the greater good of the community, held his tongue when stern clarification were probably deserved, and lived in a genuine wholesomeness of integrity. It's been the mantra of his life.

 That opens doors for my siblings and myself, plus it motivates me to live the same before my kids, my grandbabies, and my spiritual sons and daughters. That's how it's supposed to work, after all.

In The Pages

What attributes in your parents, mentors, or other influences do you aggressively pursue and incorporate into your lifestyle? When was the last time you said "thank you" for the way they live their lives?

Handcuffs

September 21
Proverbs 21

"The way of a guilty man is crooked, but as for the pure, his conduct is upright." Proverbs 21:8, NASB

This won't take long today, but I got a personal download while thinking about this verse this morning. Currently, my knickers are in a twist about how some of my friends have been treated by "ministry people". Everything in me wants to shout at the top of my lungs, "UNCLEAN, UNCLEAN, UNCLEAN!"

I prefer retaliation, I want justice, and I wish for someone on the other side of the fence to do something that looks remotely like virtue. These are the kinds of life challenges that test the real stuff in us.

The download I got this morning was this: *"Mike, I've handcuffed and bound you in honor. You'll have to submit and resign to that fact in order for you to get yourself settled back down in peace".* Yeah, I know. Got it. Thanks.

Honestly, I could care less about this download on a religiously traditional understanding of purity. I'm not really convinced that purity is obtained or validated only by conduct. I've been around church folk too long to swallow that hogwash.

Good conduct doesn't always validate a pure heart.

We know how to be "religiously" correct while still burning with other passions that are not fruits of the Holy Spirit.

Recently, a buddy and I were discussing something his dear mom used to say whenever she assessed someone's less than wise decision: *"Well bless their little heart!"* LOL! We've all heard that before, right? Of course, it's religious code that really means: *"that poor, dumb dipshit."* Oh how we paint our facades!

What I want to point out today is something I believe God was reminding me of earlier. Sometimes, people of honor are bound and handcuffed to honor... whether they like it or not.

The possibilities of vulnerable exposure and exploitation of honor's restraint is real and without limits. Those handcuffs really do a job on us, and God is totally okay with that. Those cuffs are in our possession to use as we will, but ultimately those cuffs are His. There's no use trying to get out of them. It's better to succumb to their obvious intent:

RESTRAINT

Oh yeah, one last thought. Don't think that the hassle you get because of your honor cuffs is the end of the story. God sees all. He takes note of the things that happen to His children. Eventually, the math all evens out, in heaven OR on earth.

In The Pages

Do the cuffs of honor bind you? At what cost have they held you? Have you resigned to honor, or do you waste energy defending your ways to others? How does that affect your spiritual rest and peace?

Guard Dawg

Proverbs 22
September 22

"The eyes of the Lord keep watch over knowledge..." Proverbs 22:12, NRSV

"The eyes of the Lord guard knowledge..." Proverbs 22:12, NET

I usually write early in the morning, but I've been sitting on this one most of the day today. I see images in my mind that help me understand things. Much like an American kid drifting through a Japanese anime comic book, I focus on the various pictures, not understanding the script, but trying to interpret this thing via the art.

The first image I saw today was strange. It was God with a hyperthyroid condition. Eyes bulging as He looked down over us, guiding our accumulation of information and technology. Then it dawned on me, the bulging eyes were only a symptom of His condition. Such a condition wouldn't make it easy for anyone to see clearly. Then He spoke, *"Michael, I see it all because of my omniscience, not my protruding eyes."* Ah! Got it!

The other image was that of a military guard post. One of those Marines, dressed to the nines while holding a rifle with a finely polished bayonet, marching, taking names, and kicking butt. It was a no nonsense image of a serious God... doing His thing.

I like this image, though it's not exactly what Solomon is trying to convey here. God is not on duty, looking to spoil and thwart our quests of knowledge and understanding. In fact, He might be more interested for the good than we realize.

How can we even imagine such a thing? Because He already knows all of what we're searching for and what we're working to uncover on a daily basis. He laid out the blueprint.

> **"*In the beginning God created the heavens and the earth*
> (Genesis 1:1, NASB).**

He knows the universal schematics. He wrote the codes. He was there when it all started, and He'll be there when it all ends. To Him, there really is *"nothing new under the sun"* (Ecclesiastes 1:9, NASB).

One of our daughters conceived via in vitro fertilization. We got to see a digital image of the microscopic cells, which were to be implanted within an hour of the eggs' fertilization. What human beings can do in this arena is utterly amazing!

> **But still, the best we can do is very limited.**

Something naturally "supernatural," something beyond our control, still has to happen. The fertilized cell must attach itself to the inside lining of the woman's uterus. With all of our understanding, all of our ability, all of our information, our family knew that it was all still very much in the hands of God.

We bowed in faith and leaned into His magnificent mystery and oversight. Patti and I walked away from that whole experience more in awe of His relentless power and very much aware of how little we control on this planet.

Yes, He oversees, but He has shown his willingness to open the minds and hearts of those who explore His cosmic truths. Nine months later, we got to hold this beautiful expression of the mysterious love of man and God in our arms. One He has known about from the beginning of time!

In The Pages

How comfortable are you with not having answers to mysteries in your life? What happens when you can't get an explanation? What rules your spirit—doubt and suspicion or hope and faith? Does your God paradigm allow for unanswered questions?

Easy In—Hard Out

September 23
Proverbs 23

"Give, my son, thy heart to me, and let thine eyes watch my ways. For a harlot is a deep ditch, and a strange woman is a strait pit. She also, as catching prey, lieth in wait, and the treacherous among men she increaseth." Proverbs 23:26-28, YLT

The first thought I had today (buckle up) was this:

Some things in life are easier to get into than out of!

For example: bed, obesity, smoking, volunteering, a job you hate, porn, get-rich schemes, bad relationships, credit card debt, war, wireless phone contracts, ethical debates, political arguments, technological gadgets, golf, evidently America, refurbishment of any kind, pride, a 60-month note on a new car, an offense, baby weight, selfish ambition, a sexually-transmitted disease, a family-size bag of M&Ms, Best Buy on Black Friday, and the Baptist Church (you're on the roll until He returns or you die).

Okay, so you're giggling now. But you know it's true. I'll add one more at the end of this devo.

Today's scripture warns of the seductive powers of illicit sexual attraction. I like Young's translation because of the word *"ditch."* It's a lot easier to slip into a ditch than to get out of one. Danger! Danger!

During my seminary days, my buddy Bart and I hunted ducks like a couple of people possessed! Early one morning (3:30 a.m.), we loaded up his piece-of-crap Skylark with all our gear, a gas-bloated black Labrador named Liberty, and hitched on a flat-bottom boat to boot.

We were going hunting "by God," come rain (yep, lots of it!), sleet (oh yeah!), or snow (now it's just dumb). Did you know that red clay roads that are wet and icy have a tendency to be slippery?

There we were in the middle of frikk'n nowhere, hours prior to daylight, no longer able to keep the car on its proper course. Steering became useless, so we stopped the car.

Just then, a ferocious north wind began pushing us sideways towards a very deep ditch. Liberty started whimpering while Bart and I went back and forth between crying and laughing hysterically (nervous laughter, I guess). We spent the better part of that day trying to get our car, the dog, and the boat out of that ditch. It was a nightmare!

Easy in—hard out!

Now the last one on my list is **LEGALISTIC RELIGION**. The reason it's so easy to get sucked in is because you can fake it and no one will ever know. When people get all caught up in seeing the Bible as a rulebook and other religious people applaud outward behavior, most of the stuff Jesus really cares about gets overlooked.

Love and covenant require changes on the inside. Religion rarely changes anything. Spirit people have to change all the time!

Getting into legalistic religion is easy because it rarely has to tackle this whole idea of freedom. It just keeps the old rules. It's hard to get out of legalistic religion because, quite frankly, it's just easier to stay.

Freedom just scares the hell out of most of us! So we just go to church, hide, and call it done. A real and loving relationship with our personal God places demands on us.

This truly is the heart of the Father for his sons and daughters. Here is where we find His life! The rest is just an exit to death.

In The Pages

What does your short list of "easy in - hard out" look like? How much of that is by experience? Has experience validated your knowledge? How real is your walk with God?

Intense

Proverbs 24
September 24

"Do not fret because of evildoers, nor be envious of the wicked; for there will be no prospect for the evil man; the lamp of the wicked will be put out." Proverbs 24:19-20, NKJV

Patti and I visited West Africa in 2009. We were part of a pioneering project for a missions organization we were working with at the time. Five days in that particular country was a very long five days!

The atmosphere, from the time we cleared customs upon arrival, to the time we boarded a plane to leave the country, was spiritually exhausting. As if the warfare wasn't intense enough, it seemed that social exchanges with the people were always on the verge of boiling over into something really ugly, based on the "abruptness" of the culture.

We never left the capital city, so our perspectives are based on traffic-jammed streets, shanty neighborhoods, and constant displays of need. "Normal" conversations among the people sounded like arguments. With arms flailing and veins bulging out of necks and foreheads, it was unlike anything we had ever witnessed! It was a bit much, and we found ourselves ill prepared and overwhelmed in that culture.

More recently, we just returned from Kenya. We were taken aback by the dramatic differences between the two experiences. The people in Kenya were soft-spoken, engaging, friendly, and didn't seem so . . . agitated.

While sharing a meal with another contact in Kenya, I asked him about the obvious difference. He had been to the other country I described many times.

He said,

"Pastor Mike, those guys are pushing, pushing, pushing. They are intense because they're trying to get ahead and out of their chaos. They can't let up for a second. Someone is always trying to get ahead of them, so they have to fight the fight of their lives just to stay even. It is indeed a country where God has done much, but the church and culture has forgotten that God is their provider. There is so much governmental corruption, the people can't trust outside of themselves anymore. So the pressure is on!"

WOW! That really puts things in perspective!

In light of today's text, I thought about what *"fretting"* does to us. How quickly we trade our peace for an internal agitation that steals our rest in God!

The word is **chârâh** (pronounced *khaw-raw´*), and it means *"to glow or grow warm; to blaze up of anger, zeal, jealousy: be angry, burn, be displeased, to grieve, be (wax) hot, be incensed, kindle, very wrathful."* What all of that implies is we need to chill the hell out a bit, get a massage, and settle ourselves in the soothing truth that God is our source, and He knows what we really need!

To live outside of that confidence only opens us up to taking matters into our own hands, which almost always requires some sort of self-inflicted disturbance in the spirit or the natural.

In The Pages

When you find yourself agitated by another person, what usually flows from your heart and lips? Can you let it go, or do you find yourself internally disturbed? What happens when you fixate? How do you get back to peace?

Hidden Reefs

September 25
Proverbs 25

"Like clouds and wind without rain is a man who boasts of his gifts falsely."
Proverbs 25:14, NASB

"These people are warts on your love feasts as you worship and eat together. They're giving you a black eye—carousing shamelessly, grabbing anything that isn't nailed down. They're—puffs of smoke pushed by gusts of wind; late autumn trees stripped clean of leaf and fruit, doubly dead, pulled up by the roots; wild ocean waves leaving nothing on the beach but the foam of their shame; lost stars in outer space on their way to the black hole." Jude 1:12-13, MSG

This is sad business here. Have you ever been around someone who just *had* to impress you? Where they feel the need to throw around their credentials here and there?

It's like a really bad diet drink. You take a sip, only to realize that funky aftertaste has ruined the whole experience for you. It's really awkward. And once you realize what's going on, you have to make a choice to counter-balance the conversation with your own credentials, or just power through in humility, ignoring your urge to set some of their claims straight. It's exhausting to be around such nonsense.

When I find myself in these situations, it exasperates me to the point that I don't even want to engage in the conversation anymore. Today's Proverb is bad news. It's never a good idea to boast about you, but to do it *"falsely"* just puts the nail in the coffin. It's all a relational funeral anyways!

I wish I could say that boasting only happens sporadically in the Body and never with any of the key leaders of the church. It's a nice thought, but definitely not true. The leaders and public-eye figures of the church are often the very worst! It's one of the great targets of interest of the enemies of the Church.

Jude's letter describes how the boasting of the apostates was affecting the church. Verses 12 and 13 lay out some very colorful language to describe the damage they were causing to the Body. Peterson does a beautiful job helping us see the deeper truths.

Their boasting in order to gain quick allegiance and influence was a problem. It was all promise and no delivery. They were writing checks they couldn't cash, so to speak. People were in jeopardy.

Honestly, we all need to reassess who is ultimately responsible. I say it's you and me. It's understandable why young Christians easily fall prey to such tactics. The immature (which has nothing to do with age) are usually just looking for someone, anyone, to validate them and show them some love. But, too many seasoned saints are too easily star-struck by some of the "big name" leaders. Our rejection sets us up for this kind of exchange.

Grounded sheep still need shepherds, fathers, and friends. What they don't need are a bunch of empty promises from big-gift leaders who blow in and out of town with just another glow-in-the-dark sermon.

Are they there for you when you need them to be there for you? If not, find someone else. Put yourself under the kind of leader who knows where you work, knows the names of your children, and actually cares about the stuff in your life.

In The Pages

What feeds your soul? Is it only sermons, worship, and church activity? Do you smell "sheep" on your leaders? Are they busy trying to impress you, or do they really love on you?

Losing it

September 26
Proverbs 26

"Like one who grabs a wild dog by the ears, so is the person passing by who becomes furious over a quarrel not his own." Proverbs 26:17, NET

Golf courses and airports are good places to find out what's inside a person. Mastery of either is next to impossible.

As enjoyable as golf is to millions of people, it also continuously reminds us there's always room for improvement, and perfection is fleeting. I've seen the most gentle of personalities go "nuts" over one bad shot. Okay, maybe that person was me, but you get the point.

Maintaining one's composure is a very significant part of the game. The pros have learned how to walk away from disaster and be "all there" for the next shot. Taming the head might be more important than grooving the swing.

Airports are also a hotbed of frustration. Just getting to your gate in order to board the plane is a ridiculous ordeal of hoop jumping, despite airline marketing tactics that make flying look easy. That's just silly talk right there!

Long lines, security hassles, flight delays and cancellations, all cause a series of chain reactions. Bad weather in Dallas can disrupt the entire nation's travel patterns. Fog in Atlanta causes heartburn in San Francisco. A blizzard in Minneapolis ruins vacation plans to Jamaica. I'd bet there's a lot of money to be made inside of airport drinking holes. People inside of airports are tightly wound with very short fuses.

Patti and I recently spent 26 hours in the DFW airport waiting to take a 25-minute flight to Waco. Delay after delay, cancellation after cancellation, we sat in amazement that we were so close, yet so far. You have to stay calm.

As we watched plane after plane board and de-board, we witnessed the rising tide of frustration swell among travelers. The desk agents are only the messengers, but you'd think they had personally sabotaged each and every flight. Just because Granny is getting ready to bust open a can of whupass on some poor ticket agent because Sheba, her Dramamine-induced Pomeranian is hyperventilating in its case, doesn't mean you have to jump in. Granny will settle down soon enough.

Why is there always someone who is more than happy to join the fray?

Be above it!

Think about the serious consequences of grabbing a wild dog. Yep, you are going to get yourself bitten, maybe even mauled. Most conflict is due to unbridled passion and limited understanding. You'd best keep the cuckoo in the clock, my friend. The whole world is not plotting for your personal inconvenience. I assure you.

In The Pages

Can you stay out of another person's quarrel? When tension levels rise in public, how do you react? Can you keep quiet or do you have to vent?

Gloriously Unspectacular

September 27
Proverbs 27

"Know your sheep by name; carefully attend to your flocks; (Don't take them for granted; possessions don't last forever, you know.) And then, when the crops are in and the harvest is stored in the barns, you can knit sweaters from lambs' wool, and sell your goats for a profit; there will be plenty of milk and meat to last your family through the winter." Proverbs 27:23-27, MSG

If I hear one more person tell me they're unwilling to work a certain job because it doesn't "give them life," I think I'll blow a gasket! Where in hell did we ever get the notion that work owes us an exhilarating life? I thought *He* is the one who gives us life?

"For whoever wishes to save his life will lose it, but whoever loses his life for My sake and the gospel's will save it" (Mark 8:35, NASB).

Did I miss something?

I love today's text because it totally applies to us but remains peculiarly unfamiliar at the same time. We are not an agricultural people anymore, but Wisdom is bringing us some serious revelation here.

Grow where you are planted! Faithfully pour yourself into what you have and you'll see that God will reward you. That doesn't mean it's always easy. Sometimes you have to bust your hump every day in mundane and ordinary ways.

Whether you're a housewife who lives in suburbia America and exists only to meet the unending needs of crying babies, or you're a Gogo in Swazi, feeding orphans day in and day out, it's the same work (meals, poop, nurture), just a different location. One is not more important or more spiritual than the other!

Where is "life" for the guy who sits in that tiny cubicle on the 15th floor of that (yawn) investment firm?

What about the pediatric nurse who regularly works two 10-hour shifts three times a week so her kids can go to computer camp in the summer? Where is the "life" in that?

The teacher, the construction worker, the waitress at the Burp and Groan, the yard guy, the pilot, the pastor (oh God, the pastor), the doctor, the missionary, the farmer, the cashier at Walmart . . . it's all frikk'n work! It can all be rather unremarkable, gloriously unspectacular, tediously predictable, and seemingly unending work.

Where is the "life" in any of it?

Can we just stop with the whole "doesn't give me life" talk and just say the truth: *"I don't want to do this job because it's not what I want to do. This* (fill in the blank) *is what I want to do."* Perfect! Groovy! Go do that!

"LIFE" happens when you give yours away. "LIFE" happens because it is righteous to work. "LIFE" happens when we choose to have a different attitude and a different spirit, despite the unspectacular.

You work, you pay your bills, you make your way, you educate your kids, you take your spouse out to dinner, you bless your friends; in short, you give YOU away.

We don't get to take our stuff with us when we're dead, so we might as well use it for something good now.

The opportunity to *have* life, to *be* life, to *give* life is right under our noses—here and now. But, yes, sometimes it is work! It's not always going to be glamorous, and it probably won't make the social media headlines.

Honestly, no one is going to give a Fig Newton but you. But, are you grown up enough to do it anyway? It might even be what *He* wants!

In The Pages

So the place where you work, is it a better place because you're there? Do you need to adjust your attitude and your words about your work environment? What job lasts forever? Can't get happy? Why not make a change on the inside of you?

Tender

September 28
Proverbs 28

"A tenderhearted person lives a blessed life; a hardhearted person lives a hard life." Proverbs 28:14, MSG

Your bible translation probably reads differently, but Peterson has nailed the idea perfectly. Most English translations launch from the word "fear," here.

For example, the NASB reads, *"How blessed is the man who fears always..."* The word for *"fear"* is **pâchad** (pronounced *paw-kkad'),* and in this context it means *"to be startled, stand in awe, to shake."* To me, that signifies a full awareness that something bigger and more powerful than humanity is operating in and around my life.

Our sensitivity should be heightened! Shouldn't we be sober and wide-eyed at the wonder of something supernatural and beyond our normal capacity to fully comprehend?

This wonderment trickles down into my attitudes and posture. My entire demeanor changes as I stand amazed before an awesome God who sees me, knows me, and understands all of what I barely see. That kind of fear is consumed with the love of God, not the wrath of His judgment.

Even the Apostle Paul said that when we understand the love of God, we don't strut around with agendas and stomp about in our own certainties (1 Corinthians 13:4-7). His love tempers us; we engage one another as God's children and embrace the uncertainties of life. As Peterson says, we become *"tenderhearted"* and blessing accompanies us as we roll through life.

A *"hardhearted"* person, on the other hand, doesn't have it so good. Take a moment and read Psalms 95:1-11. In these passages, we see what the real problem was with Israel and why they wandered around in the wilderness for 40 years.

It was because their hearts were hard.

Their lack of faith and their own stubbornness were real internal heart issues. And even though God loved them, it really ticked Him off! They moved Him out of His gracious long-suffering into an unwillingness to give them what they so desperately desired.

I get that same feeling when I crash into a hardhearted person. You know it can't be any fun carrying all that baggage around, but you get a sense they can't help themselves. They live rejected and bitter, and the peace they so desperately desire is always illusive and fleeting. That makes for a hard life.

That kind of fatigue takes a toll on the body. Many of our chronic ailments and emotional social disorders are stress-related and anxiety-produced. We do it to ourselves!

Remaining tenderhearted to the Lord means that we remain pliable and sensitive to directives that may even allow for our discomfort. But trusting that *He* might be in the very thing that is causing our discomfort is what sets us up for some serious reflection. It takes a tenderhearted person to embrace brokenness when it comes.

In The Pages

How well do you receive a disturbance to your comfort? How easily do you turn to the Lord when pain arises? Would the people around you describe you as tenderhearted? If not, what would be their assessment?

Don't Bet The Jewels

September 29
Proverbs 29

"Many seek the ruler's favor, but justice for man comes from the Lord." Proverbs 29:26, NASB

*"So look at Apollos and me as mere servants of Christ who have been put in charge of explaining God's mysteries. Now, a person who is put in charge as a manager **must be faithful**. As for me, it matters very little how I might be evaluated by you or by any human authority. **I don't even trust my own judgment on this point**. My conscience is clear, but that **doesn't prove I'm right**. It is the Lord himself who will examine me and decide." 1 Corinthians 4:1-4, NLT*

Lady Wisdom isn't telling us not to seek a ruler's favor. In Proverbs 19:6, she says, *"Many will seek the favor of a generous man, and every man is a friend to him who gives gifts."* She's simply reminding us that those rulers, leaders, rich people, or whoever, are human beings, which means there's always a chance that justice won't be served properly, and you could be the one who suffers because of it.

Power isn't always handled without partiality. Even power in the hands of "well intentioned" individuals has the potential to go awry. If you don't believe me, check today's headlines. If you're banking on man's integrity, you could be setting yourself up for disappointment. Enjoy it while you have it, but don't bet the family jewels on it. It's not an automatic.

Go read 1 Corinthians 4:1-4 again. Paul reminds the Corinthians how important it is for people with big responsibilities to be faithful in those duties. He indicates fairness, equity, and righteous stewardship.

But Paul quickly discounts his trust of man, including himself. He had a clear conscience, but that didn't give him the right to boast in his own righteousness. Why his caution?

This is the Apostle Paul, for heaven's sake! If there was ever a minister of the Gospel who had the right to expect some kind of good return from man, it would have been him. But, like his master, Paul didn't put a lot of stock in the absolute certainty of every man's intentions. There was another level of approval he was looking for. Paul knew the only source of true justice is the Lord Himself.

To be blunt about it, you and I could probably do a better job of applying this to our own lives. Every now and then, we should really dial in to see what the Lord thinks about how we're handling our affairs. Just because someone thinks highly of us, doesn't necessarily mean God automatically approves.

We have to decide which is more important to us. Eventually, His justice will trump all.

In The Pages

Are you a people pleaser? Are you motivated to do something if you think you'll get praise for it? How much stock do you put in man's praise? If you're over 30, you'll probably have a much different take on the "trustworthiness" of mankind.

Shrinkage

September 30
Proverbs 30

"A leech has twin daughters named "Gimme" and "Gimme more." Three things are never satisfied, no, there are four that never say, "That's enough, thank you!" - hell, a barren womb, a parched land, a forest fire." Proverbs 30:15-16, MSG

In May of 2011, I got to visit the boundary waters between Minnesota and Canada. I was invited to join my son-in-law, his dad, and his brother for a week of camping, canoeing, and fishing.

It was a trip of many firsts for me. I caught my first walleye and pike, saw bald eagles nesting, flying, and fishing near our camp, drank water right out of the lake (no boiling), heard loon's calling in the night, and swam in broad daylight (in extremely cold water!) wearing only my birthday suit. It was an incredible week!

The strangest of these experiences was fishing with leeches. Growing up in the south, I cut my teeth on fishing with artificial baits. I had never even seen a leech except for in the movies.

As I dug my hand into the pale to grab my bait, I was amazed with how these little vermin never stopped trying to latch on to my hand for a taste of blood. They were relentless! It was obvious these little critters had one thing on their radars: **Gimme!**

Today's lesson is about greed. Greed is the relentless pursuit of self-satisfaction, whatever the cost! This kind of selfishness shrinks our world.

Those leeches didn't care about any of the wonderful sights and sounds all around them. All of that beauty! God's majestic creation! But all they wanted was immediate self-gratification—to get what they didn't have.

They didn't even care that I was running a hook through them. They never wavered for a moment in their attempts to latch on to my arm.

The drive of greed is miserably insatiable.

That's why it's so dangerous to the Body of Christ. It doesn't give a crap about anything other than what it doesn't have.

The epistles are full of warnings about greed (Romans 1:28-32; Ephesians 5:3; Colossians 3:5; 2 Peter 2:12-15). Jesus said,

"Beware, and be on your guard against every form of greed; for not even when one has an abundance does his life consist of his possessions" (Luke 12:15, NASB).

He goes on to warn about building barns and bigger barns to store all of our possessions (Luke 12:21). It might be one of the most sobering truths Jesus ever spoke.

I honestly believe most of us only agree in principle.

When was the last time we unloaded all the unnecessary clutter in our own "barn?"

What is it that is shrinking your world?

Are you addicted to doing ministry overseas, but you won't cross the street to help your neighbor?

Is church work a selfish desire, or a real calling on your life?

The leech wants what it wants. It gives nothing away in its own small and shrunken world. There is no life in *gimme*!

In The Pages

What kind of ministry stuff (serving) are you doing that no one knows about except you and the Lord? Could you be pushing for an exotic global experience that realistically could happen today, right under your nose where you are now? How much fluffy romance is in your passions to serve God? How do you kill your own greed?

ENDNOTES

July 29 – [1]Tozer, A. W. *The Pursuit of God.* (Public Domain). Tozer's biographer, James L. Snyder had these comments about Tozer: *"His preaching as well as his writings were but extensions of his prayer life."* Snyder adds, *"He had the ability to make his listeners face themselves in the light of what God was saying to them."*

August 17 – [2]Patti and I visited the grave of Specialist Ross A. McGinnis at Arlington National Cemetery in July 2012. You can't explain the feeling of being on such hallowed and sacred soil. It's overwhelming. I'll never forget the experience.

September 4 – [3]The line was from the 2nd *Matrix* movie. *Matrix: Reloaded* (2003) Warner Bros Entertainment, Inc.

RESOURCES

BIBLE KEY:

<u>KJV</u> - *The Holy Bible, King James Version* (Public Domain).

<u>MSG</u> – Peterson, E. H. (2005). *The Message: the Bible in contemporary language.* Colorado Springs, CO: NavPress. Used by permission.

<u>NASB</u> - *New American Standard Bible: 1995 update.* (1995). LaHabra, CA: The Lockman Foundation. Used by permission.

<u>LXX</u> - Brenton, L. C. L. (1870). *The Septuagint Version of the Old Testament: English Translation.* London: Samuel Bagster and Sons.

<u>NCV</u> - *The Everyday Bible: New Century Version.* (2005). Nashville, TN: Thomas Nelson, Inc. Used by permission.

<u>NET</u> - Biblical Studies Press. (2006). *The NET Bible First Edition; Bible. English. NET Bible.; The NET Bible.* Biblical Studies Press. Used by permission.

<u>NIV</u> – *THE HOLY BIBLE, NEW INTERNATIONAL VERSION®.* Copyright © 1973, 1978, 1984 by International Bible Society. Used by permission.

<u>NKJV</u> - *The New King James Version.* (1982). Nashville: Thomas Nelson. Used by permission.

<u>NLT</u> - *New Living Translation* (1996, 2005, 2007). Tyndale House Publishers, Inc., Carol Stream, Illinois 60188. Used by permission.

<u>NRSV</u> - *The Holy Bible: New Revised Standard Version.* (1989). Nashville: Thomas Nelson Publishers. Used by permission.

<u>RSV</u> - *Revised Standard Version of the Bible*, copyright 1952 [2nd edition, 1971] by the Division of Christian Education of the National Council of the Churches of Christ in the United States of America. Used by permission.

<u>TLB</u> – *The Living Bible* (1971) Tyndale House Publishers, Inc., Wheaton, IL 60189. Used by permission.

<u>YLT</u> - *The Young's Literal Translation Bible* (Public Domain).

OTHER HELPS:

Baxter, J. Sidlow (1960). *Awake My Heart*. Copyright © 1960. Zondervan Publishing Company, Grand Rapids, MI.

Blue, J. R. (1985). James. (J. F. Walvoord & R. B. Zuck, Eds.)*The Bible Knowledge Commentary: An Exposition of the Scriptures*. Wheaton, IL: Victor Books.

Chambers, Oswald (1935). Original edition © 1935. *My Utmost For His Highest.* Dodd, Mead & Company, Inc., New York, NY.

Jamieson, R., Fausset, A. R., & Brown, D. (1871). *Commentary Critical and Explanatory on the Whole Bible*. (Public Domain).

Keil, C. F., & Delitzsch, F. (1996). *Commentary on the Old Testament*. Peabody, MA: Hendrickson.

Peterson, Eugene H. (2007). *Conversations: THE MESSAGE with It's Translator.* Copyright © 2007 by Eugene H. Peterson. All rights reserved. THE MESSAGE Numbered Edition copyright © 2005. NavPress Publishing Group, Colorado Springs, CO.

Rohr, Richard. *Adam's Return: The Five Promises of Male Initiation.* Copyright © 2004. Crossroad Publishing Company, New York, NY. Used with permission.

Rohr, Richard. Preparing for Christmas: Daily Meditations for Advent. Copyright © 2008. Franciscan Media, Cincinnati, OH. Used with permission.

Rohr, Richard and Feister, John. *Radical Grace: Daily Meditations by Richard Rohr.* Copyright © 1995. St. Anthony Messengers Press, Cincinnati, OH. Used with permission.

Ryrie, Charles Caldwell (1995). *The Ryrie Study Bible, New American Standard*: with introductions, annotations, outlines, marginal references, harmony of the Gospels, synopsis of Bible doctrine, index of Scripture, index to notes, concordance, maps, and timeline charts, and many other helps. Expanded edition. Scripture taken from the NEW AMERICAN STANDARD BIBLE®, Copyright© 1960, 1962, 1963, 1968, 1971, 1972, 1973, 1975, 1994 by the Lockman Foundation. Used by permission.

Strong, J. (2009). *A Concise Dictionary of the Words in the Greek Testament and The Hebrew Bible*. Bellingham, WA: Logos Bible Software.

Thomas, R. L. (1998). *New American Standard Hebrew-Aramaic and Greek dictionaries : updated edition*. Anaheim: Foundation Publications, Inc.

Thomas, R. L., The Lockman Foundation. (1998). *New American Standard exhaustive concordance of the Bible: updated edition*. Anaheim: Foundation Publications, Inc.

ACKNOWLDEGEMENTS

I would be remiss if I didn't thank some people. Patti Paschall, the love of my life, is the one who prodded me the most to start putting my thoughts on paper. For over 35 years, she's been the one to lead the charge to encourage me. No one has believed in me more. Her "I love this" has been quite the life source. She is my Jesus with skin. She has everything to do with my finishing this project. I can't imagine such a venture without her being beside me. My one, my only, my queen. xo

My children and grandchildren also provide the most amazing motivation to spill the goods. My girls and their guys are spiritually very serious and engaged. They're on the edge, and they push me to peak over their ledge from time to time. I love their views. Nicole, Steve, Paige, and Jon: I could not be more blessed by you. xo

One thought that really helped me chill out and be real was the idea that one day my grandbabies will be Kingdom fire-breathers. They'll be much more aggressive in the Spirit than myself, but maybe there is enough here to feed them for a season or two. Isabel Rose, Jones Michael, Lewis Christian, Grace Irene, and those to follow: you are perfection in my heart! xo

I wrote and compiled the first month of devos in January 2010 and presented them to 18 of my intimate peers. I asked them for honest feedback. A few did indeed respond, but the majority never said a word. To those few who did respond, I got some major encouragement. Thank you.

In fact, it was my son-in-law, Jon, who drove the decisive nail when he asked me, *"Ba, who is your audience?"* Baaamm! I knew this project wasn't necessarily going to be for "church people." Anyone was welcome to read it, and I was totally fine with that, but the people Patti and I were mentoring as we traveled the globe were the audience that pulled on my heart. I wanted to talk to young men and women who were not hung up in some sort of religious system. From that point on, it was game on. Whether or not I accomplished that with this devo is yet to be seen.

I had a group of people I called the "Devo Club," who read the stuff I was emailing them weekly. Their faces were the ones I pictured when I was writing. Some of them periodically commented and offered suggestions. All of them encouraged me to keep going forward. Taryn Mast, Rocio Doyle, Darci Simpson, Jennifer Goeddertz, Megan Dietrich, Sara Hansen, Dennis

Gable, Sarah Lapp Clements, Ashley Higgins, Erika Baldwin, and Kellen Gorbett. Thanks guys! I love you people dearly!

But there were two other members of the Devo Club who gave me feedback on a daily basis. Kayla and Andrea journaled their responses to each day's lesson and basically allowed me to peek into their hearts as they were processing the material. I can't even begin to explain how that kept me going!

Kayla Phillips Hindes was the voice of an angel. She reeks of encouragement anyway, but she really honed her craft when I needed it the most! Thanks baby. I'll owe you forever.

Andrea Gosselin jumped in during the editing process. She made her deeply vulnerable thoughts available to me on a daily basis. What a gift you are, woman! I love what you have with the Lord!

I have had two editors with this project, Erika and David. Erika Baldwin is a true spiritual daughter, but also an amazing wife to Bradley and a committed mother to Hannah and Luke. What it cost her to edit this project is a debt I'll never be able to repay. The Lord spoke clearly to me that she was to be my editor long before I asked her. Patti and I prayed hard about it. We knew this would be a drain on her family. Erika and I were in constant communication throughout the process—a time I'll always cherish. She was perfect for me. She clarified my scribbling without me having to lose my voice. That was what I wanted. That is what I got. Thanks babe! Love you! xo

David Reyes is a busy man. Too busy actually, but he volunteered to be the final eyes before we published ***RAW TALKS WITH WISDOM – Not Your Grandma's Devo***. His gorgeous wife Catherine (now carrying twins) and precious daughter Liv have patiently shared their David throughout this effort. David is a good son. He's served when he really didn't have the time or energy to do it. I'm grateful for his love and devotion. Thanks dude! xo

Once we decided to test readership with an email version of ***RAW TALKS WITH WISDOM – Not Your Grandma's Devo***, it simply would not have happened without Allison Johnston. She basically said, "I'll handle it," and that is exactly what she did. Allison would disappear for a week and then show up and say, "Look at this!" It was awesome! She also took all the pictures we used in the email version. She is the epitome of a spiritual daughter. Perfection really. Love you so much. xo

Jon Egan (my son by marriage) massaged the pics to make the images what we needed them to be. He's the one that has produced most of the graphics and set the overall ambience for the project. He also designed the cover and the Title Page. Again, he just fixed stuff. He always does. What a gift you are to God's people and to me. xo

And then there are the thousands of people who have allowed Patti and I to speak into their lives. I know what I know, and have learned what I have learned, because people were willing to ask me what I thought, and then give me space in their lives to work it out with them.

As I spoke, ministered, discipled, pastored, mentored, and tried to love, I learned a lot about people and probably even more about myself. Even when the stuff coming out of my mouth wasn't too good, most have loved on me well throughout the seasons. I do not deserve all the ways in which I have been honored. Not in the least. Thank you for your trust. I love you all.

And Lord, thank you for your patience, mercy, and unfailing love. You've changed me... from the inside out.

Thank you for everything! I am a blessed man!

Mike
2013

AUTHOR

Mike Paschall was born in Pine Bluff, Arkansas, but raised in Texas. He is a graduate of the University of Arkansas-Fayetteville with a BSEd. He also graduated from Southwestern Baptist Theological Seminary in Ft. Worth, Texas with an MDiv. Mike has served as pastor at numerous churches since 1987 and currently serves as pastor in the United Methodist Church. Mike and Patti were married in 1977. They have two daughters (Nicole, married to Steven Brewer, and Paige, married to Jon Egan) and six grandchildren (Isabel Rose, Jones Michael, Lewis Christian, Grace Irene, Esther Jane, and William Michael) who all live in Colorado Springs, CO. Mike loves any opportunity to mentor young pastors, missionaries, men and women who are passionate about ministry and Kingdom. He also loves preaching, teaching, and writing about the things of God. He is also particularly fond of a good hang with family, a cigar with a great friend, his Indian motorcycle, and an occasional trip to the golf course.

"David once told his son, Solomon, "Wisdom is the principle thing." I think every son craves a father that knows and lives that truth. Mike has taken me (and so many others) under his wing as a son and daily allowed me to grow by experiencing his wisdom, which was earned through all types of joys and sorrows. Wisdom IS the principle thing, and Mike models that by the way he lives, leads, shares and writes!" David Brown - Minister to Youth, Bella Vista Baptist Church, Bella Vista, AR.

"This devo is made most powerful by the man that lives the words every day. Mike Paschall's insights are a testament to a life worth the journey. More than a collection of daily readings--but a lifetime of wisdom, love, and challenge poured onto these pages. RAW TALKS WITH WISDOM will provoke you, inspire you, and make you scratch your head a bit. Often challenging the status quo that was lodged in my spirit, this devo led me to examine fully, wonder longer, and love deeper." - Allison Johnston - COO at Umba "an e-commerce platform for handmade goods," Atlanta, GA.

"Paschall is one of my best friends. Actually more than that, he's my priest. It's usually to him I go when I need a safe place to land my failures. I normally find brutal truth dripping with amazing grace. Regarding this book, it's become one my favorite daily meditations. Mike writes like he lives -

vulnerable, honest, and real. WARNING, this book isn't for the staunchly, overly religious, or spiritual know-it-alls. It's a devotional for regular folks, just like us..." Michael Hindes - coach, teacher, trainer, father, President of Kingdom Inc. & MRH Consulting, Atlanta, GA.

"Real, Raw, Biblical, Wise - did I say Raw? Yep - a lot like Mike, is this daily devo he's written, and it's what I love about it (and him). I've known Mike for over 25 years, and one of the things you can count in from him is that he'll tell it to ya straight - no song and dance - no shifting shadows - no wondering "what did he mean by that?" What's best, however, is that his straight talk comes from a place of wisdom, knowledge, experience, and love. There are few people in the planet whose opinion I value more, so just subscribe to the damn devo and read it! Good stuff!" David Johnson – Sr. Pastor at Church of the Open Door, author of *The Subtle Power of Spiritual Abuse*, Maple Grove, MN.

"Mike Paschall is my friend... this Devo is a frank, edgy communication of truths from the heart of God. I love Mike because of his honesty and transparency. If Jesus were talking to his disciples, or to the people of the day, I think he would smile at the conversational communications of this son. If you want a normal religious devotional reading, there are many available... but for those that have embarked on an honest difficult journey with a living Christ... I recommend Mike's Devo's... they will leave you thinking, crying, laughing and challenged." Dr. Bob Nichols - pastoral coach, counselor, teacher, Bellingham, WA

"Mike Paschall's mental and spiritual meanderings are thought provoking and interesting. Mike, who pastored mainstream churches in the past, presents a first hand account of religion, as some of us knew it, with a modern dose of common sense and the realization that all things change and deserve a re-look. Agree with Mike or not you will never be bored and his thoughts will cause you to think. Today's Christianity is due a new look and Christians owe it to themselves and others to use the critical thinking skills God gave us all." Rev. Paula Brown - A true West Texas girl, political purveyor, and forever poster-child of the 60's, Moody, TX.

"If it is real bread from God you want you have picked up the right book. Mike is a very real minister of the gospel that knows what you need when you wake up and you are starving for God to give you a Word for your life. Mike will blast you in the heart with his unique gifted use of language. Mike is one of the most important friends I have in the world. I have known Mike for over twenty-five years as one of my accountability friends. When I need a word from God, in a language that can only come from the Holy Spirit, I call

Mike. He is truly gifted with speaking a tongue that you will understand. His devotional guides will guide you to the throne of God." Bart McMillan – Business Chaplain, President of Life's Lesson's Ministries, Gainesville, GA.

"As someone who has rarely done daily devotions, I did not know if I would keep up or stick with it. I've done both, and have thoroughly enjoyed and benefited from these daily "nuggets" of wisdom. These writings are insightful and thought provoking. I look forward to my devotion time every day." David Taylor - Senior Academic Consultant at a large private university, married father-of-two, McGregor, TX.

"Mike's devotionals are open, honest and refreshing. But most of all they are unfiltered by the spirit of "religion" that has invaded so much of biblical teaching in the world today. His desire for us to know the real Jesus is apparent in all that is included in this work. Whether you are a committed follower of Jesus Christ or seeking in your spiritual journey, I recommend this book for you." Barry Strickland - Texas Director of New Wilderness Adventures, Lancaster, TX.

"One of the characteristics of Mike Paschall that I greatly respect is his direct approach. He has a gift for unpacking principles and truths from God's Word and putting them in down-to-earth and in-your-face words that make it impossible to wiggle away from their weightiness. In RAW TALKS WITH WISDOM, Mike shares a daily dose of truth, without the sugar coating, that will lead you to a deeper relationship with God." Stephanie Pridgen - Missionary Church Administrator for International Christian Assembly, Kiev, Ukraine.

"Nothing strikes of more importance to me than 'a real Christian' and by that I mean a raw, lay it out on the table, I've made mistakes, and this is who I am Christian. We are called to make disciples and I truly believe we can't do that until we are real with each other. And that is why RAW TALKS WITH WISDOM is truly amazing. They are as real and raw as it gets. I truly believe the "church" is afraid to talk that way, but through Mike and his devos I have been able to face obstacles that I can assure you are not pretty or clean, but that is life and thank God somebody like Mike is not afraid to speak right to the heart of what life is really all about!" Taryn Mast – Performance Coach, San Diego, CA.

"To know Mike is to love him dearly or not at all, mostly because he leaves very little margin for misunderstanding. RAW TALKS WITH WISDOM is beautiful for that very reason; it is a heartfelt journey through the book of Proverbs that will lead you gracefully into a deeper relationship with

Wisdom. 'In The Pages' offers an opportunity for each reader to work through the details as their story collides with God's story through the scriptures. If you are looking for a devotional that will make you feel safe, this isn't it. If you're searching for a daily opportunity to be honest with yourself and with God, then dive in... just keep in mind, this isn't your grandma's devo!" Dennis Gable – A multi-faceted, uniquely gifted Kingdom communicator who lives with his gorgeous wife and beautiful children in Phoenix, AZ.

www.ingramcontent.com/pod-product-compliance
Lightning Source LLC
Chambersburg PA
CBHW021950290426
44108CB00012B/1010